KNOWING SIN

SIN

SEEING A NEGLECTED DOCTRINE THROUGH THE EYES OF THE PURITANS

MARK JONES

MOODY PUBLISHERS

CHICAGO

Some content in the section "Imputed Guilt" in chapter 2 was adapted from Joel R. Beeke and Mark Jones, *A Puritan Theology: Doctrine for Life* (Grand Rapids: Reformation Heritage Books, 2012), chapter 13.

Scripture quotations are from the *ESV® Bible (The Holy Bible, English Standard Version®)*, Copyright © 2001 by Crossway, a publishing ministry of Good News Publishers. Used by permission. All rights reserved.

Edited by Cheryl Molin
Interior design: Ragont Design
Cover design: Studio Gearbox
Cover image of landscape copyright © 2020 by Martins Vanags / Shutterstock (401914630). All rights reserved.

Library of Congress Cataloging-in-Publication Data

Names: Jones, Mark, 1980- author.
Title: Knowing sin : seeing a neglected doctrine through the eyes of the Puritans / Mark Jones.
Description: Chicago : Moody Publishers, [2021] | Includes bibliographical references. | Summary: "The first rule of combat is: know your enemy. When it comes to sin, it's vital to know what you're up against. Mark Jones collects the insights of the Puritans about sin into a single volume. The result is a surprisingly relevant book that you'll refer to again and again"-- Provided by publisher.
Identifiers: LCCN 2021038729 (print) | LCCN 2021038730 (ebook) | ISBN 9780802425195 | ISBN 9780802476555 (ebook)
Subjects: LCSH: Sin--Christianity. | Puritans--Doctrines.
Classification: LCC BT715 .J66 2021 (print) | LCC BT715 (ebook) | DDC 241/.3--dc23
LC record available at https://lccn.loc.gov/2021038729
LC ebook record available at https://lccn.loc.gov/2021038730

Originally delivered by fleets of horse-drawn wagons, the affordable paperbacks from D. L. Moody's publishing house resourced the church and served everyday people. Now, after more than 125 years of publishing and ministry, Moody Publishers' mission remains the same—even if our delivery systems have changed a bit. For more information on other books (and resources) created from a biblical perspective, go to www.moodypublishers.com or write to:

Moody Publishers
820 N. LaSalle Boulevard
Chicago, IL 60610

3 5 7 9 10 8 6 4 2

Printed in the United States of America

Praise for *Knowing Sin*

In this book, the author of *Knowing Sin*, steeped in the tradition of the Puritans, teaches us not only the *what* and *whence* of sin, but also *how* the faith, hope, and love given to us by the Father in Jesus Christ and sealed upon our hearts by the Holy Spirit guide us in the daily mortification of sin. I know of no other contemporary volume on sin that sets forth orthodox doctrine with such precision while searching the heart of the reader at such depth.

Shao Kai "Alex" Tseng, Department of Philosophy, Zhejiang University, China

Sin: the reality of its universality is evident to all, yet modern men and women so frequently refuse to own up to this hard-core fact of human existence. But what is even more devastating is that far too many professing Christians today downplay the seriousness of what the Puritans rightly regarded as the plague of sin. In this incisive examination of what these very same Puritans can teach us about sin, Mark Jones has produced a much-needed, solidly biblical study for our modern dilemma of ostrich-like denial. A necessary read!

Michael A. G. Haykin, chair and professor of church history, The Southern Baptist Theological Seminary

In a world where depressing news abounds, why pick up a book that tells us how bad we really are? After reading Mark Jones's *Knowing Sin*, the answer will be obvious: because we need to. *Knowing Sin* made me uncomfortable. It's methodically specific. It's agonizingly comprehensive. It's personal. It's unrelenting. And it's biblical. Aided by some long-departed Puritan friends, Mark identifies the origins of our sin problem, clears up a multitude of MISUNderstandings about sin, gives us fresh reasons to hate sin's sinfulness, and opens our eyes to sins we should be fighting but are probably ignoring. Most importantly, he leads us to embrace the joyful truth that forgiveness and righteousness are found in Christ's perfect life, substitutionary death, and triumphant resurrection alone. I've pondered and quoted Mark's book to others for weeks, and expect I'll do so for years to come. It's that good.

Bob Kauflin, director of Sovereign Grace Music

You need this book as much as I do. We both need this book because we are both sinners, both natural haters of God and haters of our fellow man. If we are to obey God's call on our lives to put sin to death and come alive to righteousness, we must wage war against that mortal enemy, sin. But to successfully battle our enemy we need to know our enemy. In the pages of this book, you will come to know sin, learn to hate it even more, and learn why (and how) you must become free from its captivity.

TIM CHALLIES, blogger, author, and book reviewer

I genuinely think that *Knowing Sin* will be the most critical book that faithful Christians will be reading for many years to come.

ROSARIA BUTTERFIELD (from the foreword), homeschooling mother and writer, author of *The Secret Thoughts of an Unlikely Convert*, *Openness Unhindered*, and *The Gospel Comes with a House Key*

What doctor would receive our respect if he offered a cure without a careful diagnosis? Yet we shy away from a thorough diagnosis of the deadly illness of our souls—the inward evil of sin. Mark Jones takes God's holy Word, which penetrates and reveals with far more accuracy than any medical scan, and shows us the heinousness of sin so that we may find healing from the Great Physician. This book draws from the biblical wisdom of the Puritans and other classic Reformed writers to offer radical insight into the nature of sin and a great help to those who want to mortify the enemy within.

JOEL R. BEEKE, President, Puritan Reformed Theological Seminary, Grand Rapids, MI

Reading *Knowing Sin* by Mark Jones was difficult, though not at the fault of the author. Indeed, Dr. Jones is a clear writer whose pithy and memorable turns of phrase make this a book that is easy to digest. He is also an excellent interpreter of the Puritan tradition and uses those sources with great effect. The problem with the book has more to do with me, the reader. Reading about my own sin and the impact it has both on myself and those I love brought with it conviction. This is the greatest benefit of Dr. Jones's insights, that the gospel is a true balm to sin-weary souls. I'm very thankful that this book is being published, and I pray that it will have its desired result in the church as Christians live lives of constant repentance before a very merciful God.

IAN CLARY, Assistant Professor of Historical Theology at Colorado Christian University, Lakewood, CO

Dedicated to Joel & Emily Tiegreen

CONTENTS

FOREWORD

"The mind is its own place, and in itself / Can make a Heaven of Hell, a Hell of Heaven," so declares the fictional Satan of seventeenth-century John Milton's magisterial epic poem, *Paradise Lost*. Theologians, philosophers, and poets have all found sin and the father of sin, Satan, obsessively fascinating topics. So damning was Adam's sin in the garden that the whole creation now groans under it. Minimizing this sin (how can eating fruit be wrong?), blaming God (how cruel of God to put temptation before Adam), or renaming this sin as grace (how exciting sin has made life) pervade our age.

The key to not following Satan off of this cliff of our own making is to know sin—to know it thoroughly. Knowing Christ (which is also the title of a previous outstanding book by Mark Jones) requires that we know sin. Born of sin (Psalm 51), we consistently sin against God, others, and ourselves, sometimes simultaneously. Sin is our first language. Because of this, we need additional help to see it, hate it, repent of it, fight it, and flee from it. Indeed, the Christian's daily task is to hate your sin without hating yourself and drive a hundred fresh nails into your indwelling sin every day.

But, really now, does anyone believe this anymore?

Repenting of sin, or "repentance unto life" as rendered in the

Westminster Confession of Faith, has fallen on hard times. The thinking goes like this: if love = love, then Jesus can't hate sin. If Jesus is compassionate, then He sees my sin from my point of view, not the Bible's: Jesus knows the bad things I do are just coping mechanisms. The consequence of this unbiblical standard preached from cultural Christian pulpits and social media today is deadly. Take, for example, the #ChurchToo movement, which has recently pushed to the front line women who are repenting of their repentance. Yes, you got that. Some prominent women who had previously and publicly repented of adultery have been encouraged by the #ChurchToo movement to see their adultery as a manifestation of abuse, not sin. This (feminist) logic goes like this: If their adultery partners were older and in positions of power over them, then their sexual misconduct was a manifestation of their victimhood, not their sin. If you are a victim, you can't be a sinner, so declares the wisdom of our age. True? False. Relying on the best Puritan minds, Mark Jones shows how you can be both sinned against and sinning, all at the same time. No one wants to put sinful burdens on the backs of actual victims, least of all Mark Jones. And the most burdensome thing you can do to a true believer is bind her to theological ignorance and discourage her from repentance.

Mark Jones in *Knowing Sin* will faithfully guide you to see sin for what it is. By knowing what sin is, you will grow in discernment. You will be able to cut through the confusion of our age.

I genuinely think that *Knowing Sin* will be the most critical book that faithful Christians will be reading for many years to come. When I look at the world around us and try to make sense of our scandals and de-conversions, and as I listen to others trying to do the same, I realize that many prominent Christians are just shooting in the dark. What's missing is something found in Mark Jones's *Knowing Sin*: a thorough treatment of the distinction between the essence and the ethic of sin. Because broad evangelical culture has lost any vocabulary for the essence of sin and has redefined ethics on psychological terms, we live in a (Christian) world that locates sin in intentions, not actions. This nugget is found in chapter 3, "Sin's Privation," which might just be worth the book's price. I commend this book to you highly. May God use it to wake us up to the danger that lies both within and without, both behind and ahead. May God ready us for revival as we face the facts: our ignorance of what sin is could cost us our soul.

—**ROSARIA BUTTERFIELD**, homeschooling mother and writer, author of *The Secret Thoughts of an Unlikely Convert, Openness Unhindered,* and *The Gospel Comes with a House Key*

INTRODUCTION: ROCK YOU LIKE A HURRICANE

"Sin is the worst of Evils, the evil of evils, and indeed the only evil; nothing is so evil as, nay, nothing is evil (properly) but sin, nor in comparison of it."[1] So wrote the Puritan Ralph Venning (c. 1622–74), in his classic work on sin, *Sin, the Plague of Plagues.*

Other than knowing God, your greatest advocate, nothing else in this world is more important than knowing sin, your greatest enemy. Perhaps only the most introspective and morbid souls would venture to read a book on sin—and one so heavily influenced by the Puritans, who dealt with the topic meticulously, forthrightly, and extensively.

Yet few theological topics are as needed in the church today as the doctrine of sin (*hamartiology*). Christians should know that a proper understanding of grace requires a thorough grasp of sin. A distorted, weak view of sin will lead to a disfigured, anemic, and unproductive theology. Thomas Watson (c. 1620–86) well said, "The more bitterness we taste in sin, the more sweetness we shall taste in Christ."[2]

Some of the great displays of both God's character and His grace are revealed in the context of sin. For example, Genesis 3, Exodus 33, Psalm 51, Isaiah 53, and Romans 3 present some of clearest scriptural pictures of God and His redemptive purposes yet in connection with powerful declarations of sin. We stand to gain a lot from a book on sin when we realize the lengths to which the triune God has gone to redeem sinners. Is not the Bible a book on sin? God saves sinners, not good people (Luke 5:32).

Our sins are indeed a problem, but who we are by nature presents the real dilemma. And even in our state of grace, "there is," says Thomas Brooks (1608–80), "the seed of all sins—of the vilest and worst of sins—in the best of men."[3] In fact, Brooks adds, "there is not a worse nature in hell, than that that is in [you]; and it would discover itself accordingly, if the Lord did not restrain it."[4] No one person is better or worse than another left entirely to oneself. Only God makes us to differ.

Who are you? This book may help you answer that question more thoroughly and accurately (though, it must be said, we are merely scratching the surface on this topic). The response may make you uncomfortable, but do you wish to be honest with yourself and God? If you want to be flattered or lied to, I suggest you listen to a politician. We frequently cannot bear to take an in-depth look at our lives and hearts and the darkness that remains in them. We might think hearing the truth will be painful; but, considering the God we know and the gospel He reveals, I am confident the pain will be worth it. If David Clarkson (1622–86) is right that "He is the most faithful friend, and worthy of most esteem and affection, that deals most plainly with us, in reference to the discovery of our sin,"[5] then please receive this book as an act of love.

Finally, remember, Christ is for us, but He is for real sinners, not pretend ones. Martin Luther (1483–1546) wrote to Philip Melanchthon (1497–1560) in August of 1521, exhorting him to preach a true mercy, not an imaginary mercy. But true mercy must be preached in the context of true, not imaginary, sin. God saves real sinners, not imaginary sinners. Luther concluded his letter: "Pray hard for you are quite a sinner."

Read on, for you, indeed, are quite a sinner.

SIN'S ORIGINS: SYMPATHY FOR THE DEVIL

IN THE BEGINNING

The origin of sin is a fascinating but deadly serious discussion that should not be ignored by anyone wishing to understand themselves, this world, God, and the life to come. Not only Christians, but many outside of the faith recognize evil in this world and want to know where evil came from.

The Dutch theologian G. C. Berkouwer (1903–96) observed regarding the presence of sin, "No real genius is needed to see life's battered and mangled pieces before us, and no particular wisdom is required to appreciate how profoundly abnormal life can be."[1] Who, with even a cursory knowledge of world news and history, could possibly say all is (and has been) well and good?

Those who believe in a purely materialistic universe naturally face the dilemma of whether we can even speak of objective good and evil. Christians, however, believe that God rightly called His completed work of creation "very good" (Gen. 1:31). We believe God righteously determines what is good and evil because He alone is truly good (Mark 10:18). When sin entered the world through Adam, creation became, in a sense, "very bad." Another Dutch theologian, Herman Bavinck (1854–1921), remarked, "Sin ruined the entire creation, converting its righteousness into guilt, its holiness into impurity, its glory into shame, its blessedness into misery, its harmony into disorder, and its light into darkness."[2] When looking at the origin of sin we cannot appreciate its ruining effects unless contrasted with the original declaration by God Himself that what He had made was very good.

In discussing sin, we must ask two fundamental questions: Whether it be so? and What is it?

Sin is a human problem insofar as we are responsible for it. Yet the solution is not ours to produce, since, like the leopard unable to change his spots (Jer. 13:23), we cannot cleanse ourselves without God's grace. The solution to the problem of sin thus falls to God, against whom sin is ultimately committed (Ps. 51:4). He alone possesses the wisdom to find a way to bring purity out of impurity, to make beautiful what is ugly, to make straight what is crooked.

God created the context for and possibility of sin. He created man and gave him His law, including a specific positive injunction Adam was to obey: "But of the tree of the knowledge of good and evil you shall not eat, for in the day that you eat of it you shall surely die" (Gen. 2:17).

God did not elevate our first parents to a place that ruled out the possibility of sin and death. As we find out, Adam and Eve sinned by failing to conform to God's righteous requirements (Gen. 3:6). Yet in his state of integrity and innocence, Adam was able to not sin, but not infallibly or immutably so. God did not confirm Adam in a state of immutable goodness, as He does with us when we are united to His Son and possess the Spirit of holiness (Rom. 8:9–11), which will only be fully realized in glory.

Adam's fall resulted from two major causes: one internal (his own free will) and one external (the devil). With the latter in mind, the origin of sin among humans must take into consideration the same among the angelic host. There was an "Evil One" who tempted Adam and Eve into sin.

SATAN'S FALL

The serpent appears in Genesis 3 but without a background offered for his presence in the garden. The unfolding of God's revelation gives us more information, but the snake plotting to deceive the woman into disobedience against God may take us by surprise at first. We find out later that the fall on earth among men was preceded by another fall in a spiritual realm among angels. Here we encounter one who took part in that fall and who arrives on the scene as the consummate enemy against God: "Satan" (Hebrew), also called "the devil" (Greek) (John 8:44; 1 John 3:8).

In the garden, the serpent not only murders, but lies in order to do so. Jude tells us of the angels who "did not stay within their own position of authority, but left their proper dwelling" (v. 6). In other words, before Adam and Eve sinned, sin originated among the angels. The issue seems to have been one of a struggle over authority, the very matter that led to Adam's fall. In *On the Fall of Satan*, Anselm of Canterbury (1033–1109) argued that the devil set his will against God as an attempt to be God's equal. This, again, speaks to authority. Understanding something of the fall of Satan—though even Anselm's explanation is not altogether fully satisfactory—helps us grasp the fall of man.

Paul seemed to suggest that pride was involved in the devil's willing apostasy from God in 1 Timothy 3:6: "He must not be a recent convert, or he may become puffed up with conceit and fall into the condemnation of the devil." The devil may have turned from his affectionate contemplation of the divine majesty and focused instead upon his own glory, which led to pride and rebellion. When Satan tempted our Lord to worship him, we may be witnessing his vain quest to snatch the honor and glory that belongs to God alone. What better way than to have God Himself bow down to him? This was an incalculable evil desired by the devil, for he wanted Christ, filled with the Spirit, to deny Himself and His Father and affirm the devil as Lord of all.

Along with a third of the angels (Rev. 12:4), Satan fell, never to be the object of God's mercy but instead His holy wrath. The will of each angel was operative in their rebellion as they turned from good to evil of their own volition.

Satan is the "tempter" (Matt. 4:3; 1 Thess. 3:5; 2 Tim. 2:26), a conniving murderer full of "schemes" (Eph. 6:11), an opportunist (Eph. 4:27) who looks to devour (1 Peter 5:8), a prosecutor (Job 1:6–12; 2:1–5) who accuses (Zech. 3:1–2), and one who incites to sin (1 Chron. 21:1). But ultimately the "ancient serpent, who is called the devil and Satan, the deceiver of the whole world," will be publicly defeated with his accusations against God's people coming to an end (Rev. 12:7–10).

Notwithstanding the risen Christ's conquest over him, we still read of a certain type of power exercised by Satan and his angels in this world, albeit weakened because of Christ's ascension (Eph. 4:8). The power of darkness (Luke 22:53) is no doubt tied to Satan as the ruler of this world (John 12:31). Those outside of Christ belong to the "prince of the power of the air, the spirit that is now at work in the sons of disobedience" (Eph. 2:2). He blinds the hearts and minds of unbelievers (2 Cor. 4:4), oppresses many (Acts 10:38), thwarts missionary activity (1 Thess. 2:18), and casts people into prison (Rev. 2:10). In the case of Judas, Satan put it into his heart to betray Christ (John 13:2), and even entered into him (John 13:27). No one can accuse the devil of laziness; he is a vicious and persistently hard worker, who throws "flaming darts" at God's people (Eph. 6:16).

ADAM'S TRANSGRESSION

Adam and Eve were up against a formidable foe. The serpent "was more crafty than any other beast of the field that the LORD God had made" (Gen. 3:1), and devotes his life to destruction of all that is good. If he despised God's authority first, he cared even less for Adam's authority in the garden later. He wanted Adam to reject God's authority, and thus he urged him to doubt God's word and threat (Gen. 3:1, 4). Pride arose out of Adam's unbelief (Gen. 3:5). The man and the woman, by their subsequent actions, chose to believe a lie over God's revealed truth. Like the devil, Adam in apostasy turned his thoughts away from God to himself and his own glory. In this manner, we see that the apostasies of the devil and Adam bear similarities.

Adam's transgression was against the whole of God's moral law, which was written on his heart as one made in God's image (Gen. 1:27). His unbelief and pride revealed self-love, self-seeking, and self-promotion, which are violations of the first commandment. As the prophet, priest, and king of God's garden-temple, Adam was bound to worship God in a specific manner, which includes both what he should and should not do. By eating from the forbidden tree, he transgressed proper worship laws. In addition, he tolerated false religion in the temple and did not, as the guardian, destroy the works of the devil. In these ways he broke the second commandment. As God's image-bearing son, Adam was obligated to bring honor upon his Father through holy living. Adam failed to revere the word not only engraved on his heart but also spoken to him directly. This rejection of God's word constituted a dismissal of God's name and so a violation of the third commandment. Adam's disobedience also threatened his and his wife's participation in the eternal Sabbath rest (see Heb. 4:11) as they sought rest outside of God. He thus transgressed the fourth commandment and placed the eternal state of his posterity in jeopardy.

As far as the so-called second table of the law is concerned,

Adam failed to honor his Father (against the fifth commandment) in the garden, forfeiting "long days." Instead of providing life for his descendants, he brought death through sin as a murderer not unlike the devil (against the sixth commandment). Adam neglected to love and protect his wife with a proper sense of jealousy by allowing her to be entertained by the devil (against the seventh commandment). Eve subsequently stole from God in taking the forbidden fruit (against the eighth commandment) while Adam not only did nothing to prevent it but also took himself. Adam failed to counter the devil's lies and Eve's reception of them with the truth (against the ninth commandment), acting rather in the likeness of the father of lies (John 8:44). Finally, being discontent with his own estate and blessings from God, Adam coveted what did not belong to him (against the tenth commandment).

Thomas Watson offers a slightly different, but complementary, approach to Adam's sin. Quoting Cicero on parricide (i.e., the killing of a parent), the person guilty of it commits multiple sins in one. So in Adam's case, he was guilty of incredulity (disbelief), unthankfulness, discontentment, pride, disobedience, vain curiosity, wantonness, sacrilege, murder, and presumption.[3]

The above displays the evil in Adam's transgression, which was ultimately a sin against God but in the particulars a rejection of the entire law of God (James 2:10–11). Or to put it as the old theologians used to, sin is an attempted murder on God (i.e., deicide). It was also a homicide against humanity, since it made his descendants guilty.

UNDE MALUM?

As mentioned earlier, many inquire about the origin of sin in line with the question, *Unde malum?* (Whence evil?). We begin with the simple recognition that we sin because we are sinners. But related to perfectly created angels and humans, we are left wondering how such beings could freely choose to do evil. Some heretics (e.g., Pelagians and

Socinians) and others (e.g., Remonstrants/Arminians) suggest that Adam possessed an inclination to vice before the fall, though not to the extent that we do afterward. This jeopardizes the legitimacy of God's "very good" creation. Adam, prior to the fall, possessed only a desire to love and worship his Father, which is incompatible with the opposite.

So how do we make sense of sin? We need to understand that God created Adam and Eve in a changeable (mutable) state with regard to both their being and their will. Adam's fall proves that somehow he could potentially sin in his state of righteousness and holiness.

The freedom of Adam's will was a gift from God, but as is often the case even now in our post-Fall context, many blessings can become curses. Adam was presented with a false theology and entertained it. By grace, God gave Adam an innate power to not sin. However, God did not grant what we sometimes call the "grace of perseverance" that would have prevented Adam from sinning. In this way, Adam possessed *the ability to not sin* but not *the inability to sin*. We can say that God's goodness toward Adam necessitated giving sufficient grace to not sin but not the grace of perseverance to keep him from sinning. God was just in His creation of Adam, not requiring of him beyond what he was bound to offer.

The internal cause of the Fall was Adam's free will; the external (instrumental) cause was Satan's temptation. Or, as Thomas Watson says, "the devil could not have forced him unless he had given consent. Satan was only a suitor to woo, not a king to compel."[4]

God could have granted Adam the gift of perseverance and kept him from sinning. God allowed sin, because He, according to Augustine (354–430), "judged it better to bring good out of evil than not to permit any evil to exist."[5] Yet we still find ourselves groping in the dark concerning sin's origin. There seems to exist no logical or rational explanation for the origin of sin. The high-handed rebellion of Adam and Eve makes no sense to us. Perhaps this is why God does not reveal to us the inner workings of why Adam did not simply cast the serpent out of the garden. Rather, we are told of the fact of the transgression and the effects that resulted thereon.

Should we conclude that sin occurred outside of God's control? Or that a sovereign God was the author of Adam's sin? Both of these are ideas we cannot tolerate. Indeed, we reject the idea of a disinterested or an impotent God, in favor of One who is not only sovereign but good and wise in His exercise of power.

The providence of God includes His works, which are "most holy, wise, and powerful preserving, and governing all his creatures; ordering them, and all their actions, to his own glory" (Westminster Larger Catechism, A. 18). As is true of all things in this world, the fall occurred under the providence of God. He knew it would happen and ordained that it would. God declares "the end from the beginning" (Isa. 46:10), yet He can never be held accountable for anyone's sin (James 1:13). But whatever we affirm about the freedom of Adam's will and the holy providence of God, we cannot ascribe to God even the tiniest hint of wrongdoing.

Someone will say, but how can we say God ordained sin and yet held Adam responsible? This is where we must content ourselves with not going beyond what is revealed in the Scriptures. God carries out everything "according to the counsel of his will" (Eph. 1:11), and yet He holds Adam and all others responsible for their sin. At this point, we must recognize that what we cannot comprehend in our finite minds can be resolved in the mind of God. For example, Peter has no problem affirming both the sovereignty of God and the responsibility of men regarding the murder of Jesus on the cross. In the same sentence (Acts 2:23), Peter declares that Jesus was "delivered up according to the definite plan and foreknowledge of God" yet "crucified and killed by the hands of lawless men."

As stated, God did not give Adam the grace of perseverance to prevent him from falling. God could have sovereignly willed Adam to resist the devil. But, for reasons unknown to us, God did not do so, according to His permissive will. We have to affirm, however mysterious it sounds, that the Fall happened by providence of God while Adam bore moral responsibility for it. As noted earlier, although the devil is the external cause of Adam's sin, the will of Adam is the internal (principal efficient) cause. Without the latter, Adam cannot be blamed; without the former, it is hard to see how Adam could have sinned.

APPLICATION

Happy guilt (*felix culpa*) has been a response by some to the origin of evil. God has allowed sin into His good creation. As the sovereign, holy Lord, He governs evil. Sin does its worst, but God always does His best because He can do no other. The presence of sin brings to light the character of God. Without sin, perhaps some of God's attributes, as revealed to us, would have been hidden away in the depths of the Godhead. One immediately thinks of His mercy. John Owen says, "The greatest evil in the world is sin, and the greatest sin was the first; and yet Gregory feared not to cry . . . 'O happy fault, which found such a Redeemer!'"[6] God draws out the highest good from sin, as only He can.

John Duncan (1796–1870) references Samuel Rutherford (1600–1661) as saying something to the effect of, "The permission of sin is adorable, the actual fact of sin is abominable. As to the *permissio*, there would certainly have been no display of some of the Divine attributes had sin not been. They would have been conserved for ever in the depths of the adorable Godhead."[7] What we have gained from God, in Christ, remains far better than what we would have gained if Adam had not fallen. Hence, we adore God and rejoice in His goodness and wisdom, for He alone is able to bring such blessing from such misery.

In this life, we may never fully understand why Adam decided to sin against God, why a good angel would turn from God in rebellion, or why a good God would allow it, much less ordain it. But we know that both Adam and Satan are held fully responsible for their sin. In the case of Adam, while he was challenged by an external cause, he was nevertheless guilty himself and without excuse before God, though he tried to make excuse (Gen. 3:12). We can be quick to blame others for our own sins, for which we alone must accept responsibility. But God does not say to Adam, "I am sorry; that was a test too great for you; it isn't your fault." We, too, must resist the temptation to be blame-shifters whether assigned to people or circumstances in the past or present. For example, a man may blame his abusive parents for his explosive anger and parents may always blame their child's circumstances for their child's misbehavior. Indeed, we can point to shaping influences as external causes for or incitements to sin. Still, we must assign responsibility for the sin to the individual committing it. We can never claim innocence when we sin or excuse ourselves from it because of some forceful external factor involved, including Satan. Let us remove from our hearts and minds such phrases as "I could not help myself," "I was unable to resist," or "the devil made me do it."

The external forces may be great, but "God is faithful, and he will not let you be tempted beyond your ability, but with the temptation he will also provide the way of escape, that you may be able to endure it" (1 Cor. 10:13).

2

SIN'S CONTAGION: BORN THIS WAY

GOD MADE MAN UPRIGHT

In the first *Lord of the Rings* movie, Aragorn, fearful of the power the ring could have over him, knowing how it affected his ancestor Isildur, hears Arwen say to him, "Why do you fear the past? You are Isildur's heir, not Isildur himself. You are not bound to his fate."

Aragorn responds, "The same blood flows in my veins. The same weakness." Aragorn's words are quite perceptive when applied to the doctrine of original sin, but Arwen's "theology" is quite off.

Many Christians have used their sanctified imagination to think about what our original parents experienced in the garden as they lived for God. Perhaps even some holy envy has accompanied our thoughts as we think of their sinlessness, even if the blessed life they enjoyed was likely short-lived. It can boggle the mind to think of being able to live without struggling with sin or its consequences. We can only hope for what we do not yet possess; but we can't remember what we never had. Adam and Eve, and later our Lord Jesus Christ, alone possessed such in this world.

In Ecclesiastes, the Preacher says, "See, this alone I found, that God made man upright, but they have sought out many schemes" (7:29). In the beginning all that God had made was declared on the sixth day to be very good, particularly the crowning point of creation: the man and the woman (Gen. 1:31). Out of His bountiful goodness and wisdom, God endowed Adam and Eve with His own image of holiness. As creatures full of happiness, comfort, and love, they would worship in Spirit and in truth. Made in the image of God (Gen. 1:27) and with knowledge of Him, Adam and Eve had the law of God written upon their hearts (Rom. 2:14–15). "God made man upright" (Eccl. 7:29), but now we are bent, mangled, and twisted.

God endowed Adam with both a natural life and a spiritual life. His natural life concerned the union of his body and soul, so that we see Adam as a body–soul composite, or a "soulish body." His spiritual life involved the communion he enjoyed with God. The natural life he possessed in innocence required a spiritual outlet. His happiness was intimately tied up with his ability for communion with God, without which he would have been miserable.

Besides creating him in righteousness and holiness, with the moral law written on his heart, God gave Adam the Holy Spirit. Thomas Goodwin (1600–1680) affirmed that the Holy Spirit "was in Adam's heart to assist his graces, and cause them to flow and bring forth, and to move him to live according to those principles of life given him."[1] We can distinguish between the Spirit given to Adam in Eden versus the Spirit (of Christ) given to us on account of Christ's mediatorial work. The Spirit given to us by Christ guarantees perseverance to glory, but Adam had no such promise while in Eden.

Bavinck spoke of the importance of the Spirit for communion with God: "[The] Holy Spirit is the author of all creaturely life and specifically of the religious–ethical life in humans. The true human who bears God's image is inconceivable even for a moment without the indwelling of the Holy Spirit."[2] Adam could not enjoy spiritual life apart from the Spirit working in him to love and serve his Father in heaven. The Spirit was a "mediator" between Adam and his Father, a bond of love between them, just as the Spirit is a bond of love between the Son and the Father.

Related to this discussion, John Owen (1616–83) argued that both Adam and Christ were positively endowed with grace. Both Adam and Christ required the Spirit, for,

> let the natural faculties of the soul, the mind, will, and affections, be created pure, innocent, undefiled,—yet there is not enough to enable any rational creature to live to God; much less was it all that was in Jesus Christ. There is, moreover, required hereunto superadded natural endowments of grace, superadded unto the natural faculties of our souls. If we live unto God, there must be a principle of spiritual life in us, as well [as] of life natural. This was the image of God in Adam and was wrought in Christ by the Holy Spirit.[3]

Owen speaks of the necessity of both natural and spiritual life in Adam, with the Spirit making the latter possible.

THE LOSS OF GOD'S IMAGE

Sin brought the loss of these supernatural gifts and the marring of the image of God. We became idolaters, for every sin is idolatry, "an implicit adoration of Satan," says Stephen Charnock (1628–80), whereby, with the loss of God's image, we cannot offer God the worship and reverence that is due to Him.[4]

The one sin of Adam defiled us in an instant, totally—in the sense that no human faculty is left unaffected. Thus, Paul says to the Ephesians they are to "put on the new self, created after the likeness of God in true righteousness and holiness" (Eph. 4:24). Being created in the likeness of God involves regaining the true righteousness and holiness lost in the Fall. Paul likewise needed to exhort Christians to "put off your old self," because of the corruption gained in the Fall and intimately experienced in their life outside of Christ (Eph. 4:22). Original righteousness lost meant corruption found.

God's threat of death is not simply physical death. Man possesses both moral and physical faculties. Morally, sin made Adam both guilty and polluted. His guilt meant he (and his descendants) contracted the wrath of God. Additionally, his pollution meant he was universally corrupted or "totally depraved." While we are not as evil as we could be, we are so polluted that no true goodness can be found anywhere in us. Physically, Adam experienced what some call the "death of disaster." This involves the miseries we experience in this world, such as sickness, disease, deteriorating health, and the toils and frustrations of our labor. This culminates in physical or temporal death as proof that God's threat was not in vain.

Losing the image of God must, however, be understood not to mean a complete loss so that humans are now no different than animals. Historically, Reformed theologians have distinguished between the image of God broadly and narrowly considered. Narrowly it is lost with sin, but broadly it is ruined but not altogether lost. In a sense, a warped vestige remains. We still can say, despite sin, we are made in the image of God. Accordingly, the death penalty in Genesis 9:6 is based on the illegitimate murder of a person made in God's image,

> "Whoever sheds the blood of man,
>   by man shall his blood be shed,
>   for God made man in his own image."

James urges his readers to watch their tongues and laments that some Christians can both bless God and curse others who are made in the likeness of God (James 3:9). The Fall meant Adam lost his holiness, which was dependent upon the Spirit for its acceptability. God was his highest end, but now he and all people make themselves their own end apart from God. In our nature, we are now born without innate goodness and instead with a universal (i.e., all faculties) bent toward evil. We are blind and live in darkness. Instead of loving God, as we ought, we hate God (Rom. 8:7). What explains this animosity?

ORIGINAL SIN

In Romans 5, Paul states rather plainly that sin passed from Adam to all men, which led to death: "Sin came into the world through one man, and death through sin" (v. 12). After that, the details of this passage prove to be somewhat tricky and controversial. But the difficulty of the topic should not mean a retreat from the details of how and why we find ourselves in this terrible predicament involving sin. The answer to the question, "Why did we become sinners?" may be summed up in two words: Original Sin. This doctrine is, as it has been famously quipped, the only empirically verifiable Christian doctrine.[5] Even though it may be empirically verifiable, it is still highly offensive to many, even (strangely) to some in the church.

The phrase "original sin" tends to be associated with Augustine, but many of his ideas on the topic were already current among other church Fathers. There are a few reasons for the concept. It does not in the first place refer to Adam's "original" sin (a common misconception outside and inside the church), but to the sin of his descendants. Our original parents, Adam and Eve, are responsible for our sin nature. Paul makes this clear in Romans 5:12 in affirming, "Death spread to all men because all sinned," which is aptly summed up in *The New-England Primer*, "In Adam's fall, we sinned all."[6] Original sin refers not to a voluntary act committed by Adam or us but denotes what we received from him and possessed before we ever did anything. We are formed in our mothers' wombs as sinners and stand guilty before

God the moment we are conceived. As we have our being, we have our being as sinners.

Original sin explains why all actual evil in the world exists. From our corruption issues corrupt acts, as a bad tree brings forth bad fruit (Matt. 7:17–18). The explanation for Genesis 6:5, "Every intention of the thoughts of [man's] heart was only evil continually," is original sin. Watson says our heart is "*Officina diaboli*, 'the devil's shop or workhouse,' where all mischief is framed."[7] There is a mesmerizing evil genius in us all—a sinful heart, capable of imaginations we cannot speak of.

The Westminster Shorter Catechism answers Question 18 this way in describing original sin: the sinful estate of man "consists in the guilt of Adam's first sin, the want [i.e., lack] of original righteousness, and the corruption of his whole nature, which is commonly called Original Sin; together with all actual transgressions which proceed from it."

This doctrine cannot be denied without serious consequences to the Christian religion, for its denial leads to Pelagianism and the disintegration of the person and work of Christ. The old Pelagians admitted Adam injured himself through his sin, but said his descendants were not hurt in any way by it. For them, Romans 5:12ff. reflected merely our (free) imitation of Adam.

The idea that children in the womb are born "in sin" may seem hard to believe until, of course, one raises a child, and especially multiple children. If they are born without sin, what explains their early perversities? What explains their tantrums, self-centeredness, lying, stealing, domineering, and emotional manipulation (just to name a few manifested traits)? Why would innocent children do things that are hard to fathom? Christianity explains that children, even from the earliest age, manifest such sinful traits because they are born sinners (Ps. 58:3). In Psalm 51, the adulterous and murderous David recognizes his sins before getting to the root of the issue:

> Behold, I was brought forth in iniquity,
>   and in sin did my mother conceive me. (Ps. 51:5)

Notice he does not dwell on the details of his adultery or his murder of Uriah but goes right to the source of his problem. He was conceived in sin. The New Testament counterpart to Psalm 51:5 might be Ephesians 2:3, where Paul says we were all "by nature children of wrath, like the rest of mankind." As children of God's wrath, we are at fault and so punished because of a sin nature that displeases God. When a child is conceived by natural propagation, the child is constituted a sinner and is guilty before God. But, as many have pointed out, our guilt goes back to the very beginning.

IMPUTED GUILT

The Scriptures teach that sin may pass to another person or to persons in two principal ways. First, Jeroboam's false worship in 1 Kings 12 led Israel to participate with him in his sin (*participatione culpae*). They joined with him and so were guilty of false worship and idolatry. Second, sin may be passed through the guilt of imputation stemming from Adam's transgression.

It may be the case that the angels fell in a manner similar to the example of Jeroboam and the Israelites.[8] Satan led many angels into evil. He also led Adam and Eve into evil. But the worst "leading" into sin is through the guilt of Adam's first transgression.

All sins are, as Thomas Goodwin argues, "reduced unto two branches." First, "that which consists in the guilt of some act of sin done and perpetrated; or, [second], an inherent corruption in the heart contracted by that guilt."[9] When Adam sinned, both of these were true of himself. He incurred an everlasting guilt before God, which led to death. Terribly, all of Adam's natural descendants would likewise experience the same state: guilt before God and a loss of holiness. We are both guilty and defiled. Like Adam, we need the promise of God's grace in Jesus Christ (Gen. 3:15) and its application.

In the post-Reformation era, Reformed theologians continued to develop the doctrine of original sin in light of the development of covenant theology, which strongly emphasizes the two representative "giants" of world history: Adam and Christ. The actions of the first Adam have horrible consequences for his natural descendants; the actions of the second Adam (Jesus Christ) have wonderful consequences for His spiritual descendants.

The doctrine of the imputation of Adam's guilt was typically understood to provide the ground for the transmission of indwelling or inherent sin. Goodwin argued that those who speak of original sin only in terms of corruption and not also of guilt "usually . . . deny the imputation of Christ's righteousness also."[10]

One important argument for the immediate imputation of Adam's guilt was his status as a "public person." By the appointment of God, Adam and Christ were made "public persons" according to the covenants in which they represented their people, namely the covenant of works (Adam) and the covenant of grace (Christ).[11]

Romans 5 presents to us the clearest statement of both the parallel and the contrast between Adam and Christ in their representative headships. In Romans 5, two men are contrasted, one by whom sin entered the world, and one by whom it was taken away. Moreover, the comparison, Owen notes, concerns things contrary. The entrance of sin leads to its punishment, as verse 12 suggests. Because of the covenantal solidarity between Adam and the human race, all human beings—with the sole exception of Jesus Christ—have more than humanity in common with Adam. Indeed, as humanity's covenant head, Adam's sin meant that his descendants were subject to death as the punishment due for his sin. As Owen notes, they "were so by virtue of divine constitution, upon their federal existence in the one man that sinned."[12] Owen makes clear that while the Bible clearly supports the idea that through Adam's sin all men became corrupt and depraved in their natures by natural generation, nonetheless Paul's argument in Romans 5 shows that it is "the guilt of Adam's actual sin alone that rendered them all 'obnoxious' [i.e., liable] to death upon the first entrance of sin into the world."[13] The guilt of Adam's sin is imputed to the human race, and this is the principal reason that humans die.[14]

In Romans 5:12 the final clause has occasioned disagreements among theologians over the centuries. The final construct of the verse (*eph' hō pantes hēmarton*) can be translated as a causal clause, "for that all have sinned" (KJV text), or as a simple relative clause, "in whom all have sinned" (KJV margin, n. 4). The latter rendering is based on the Latin Vulgate (*in quo omnes peccaverunt*) and was preferred by John Owen in his work on justification.[15] If the marginal rendering is true, Goodwin suggests that "the matter is plain that the guilt of that his first act is the sin conveyed by imputation, and that we sinned in him."[16] Similarly, Francis Turretin (1623–87) claims, "whatever way *eph' hō* is translated, whether relatively, 'in whom' . . . or causally, it amounts to the same thing."[17]

After considering verse 12, Owen explains that death came upon all men, even upon those who did not actually sin, or sin as Adam sinned (Rom. 5:14). Therefore, the act of Adam's sin does not belong to all humans *subjectively*, but his actual sin does have consequences for his posterity because the guilt of his sin is imputed immediately to his descendants, except Christ who was not generated in the ordinary manner but supernaturally (i.e., virgin birth), and so, free from the contagion of sin. In other words, when Adam sinned, at the same time all humans sinned in Adam by representation. Hence, the imputation of Adam's guilt to his offspring was effected immediately, contemporaneous with the sin, and not mediately, that is, passed down to us when and because we sin as Adam did. As Owen argues, because of the "divine constitution" whereby we belong federally to Adam, who sinned, we are born in sin, and liable to death and punishment because the guilt of Adam's actual sin is imputed to us.[18]

The ground for our corruption is Adam's guilt imputed to us immediately because he is our covenant head.

UNIVERSALITY OF SIN

Original sin affects all people because of our foundational connection to our original parents, Adam and Eve. The story of Genesis illustrates in various ways the universal principle of sin. In perhaps the most obvious example, we are informed of man's wickedness both before the flood and after the flood. Before the flood, we read, "The Lord saw that the wickedness of man was great in the earth, and that every intention of the thoughts of his heart was only evil continually" (Gen. 6:5). After the flood, God affirms that "the intention of man's heart is evil from his youth" (Gen. 8:21). God is not unjust. He would not have killed the inhabitants of the world without good cause.

In 1 Kings 8, Solomon's prayer of dedication confesses to God, "There is no one who does not sin" (v. 46). Assuming Solomon wrote Ecclesiastes, he additionally says: "Surely there is not a righteous man on earth who does good and never sins" (7:20). Solomon evidently had the same outlook as his father, David, who advised, "Enter not into judgment with your servant, for no one living is righteous before you" (Ps. 143:2).

The New Testament only confirms this bleak view of human nature. Pulling from various Old Testament texts, the apostle Paul said in Romans 3, "None is righteous, no, not one; no one understands; no one seeks for God. All have turned aside; together they have become worthless; no one does good, not even one" (vv. 10b–12). The whole world stands accountable to God for sin (Rom. 3:19).

Those who say they are without sin are deceived (1 John 1:8). But, as Watson wrote, "We are apt to have slight thoughts of sin, and say to it, as Lot of Zoar, 'Is it not a little one?' (Genesis 19:20)."[19] Christians are often guilty of minimizing their sin, partly due to ignorance of God's law and partly due to pride. But those outside of Christ are, ironically, through their sin, unable to see the true extent and horrors of their sin nature. Most create their own hierarchies of sins: we usually are able to make the worst sins those ones we do not think we are prone to commit.

TOTAL DEPRAVITY

Few suggest they are entirely blameless. Most admit some fault in their lives, even if they minimize, excuse, rationalize, or justify in the same breath. Theological traditions have weakened the doctrine of original sin. Some affirm the loss of original righteousness while denying the universal corruption of the soul. John Calvin (1509–64) spoke truly: "We are so vitiated and perverted in every part of our nature that by this great corruption we stand justly condemned and convicted before God."[20] Calvin here highlights the extensiveness of original sin in our nature. The language of "total depravity" accurately captures the idea of what is being expressed.

Total depravity does not mean we are as sinful as we can possibly be. Otherwise, the human race would have extinguished itself a thousand times over through murder alone. But, as poison mixed in water affects every drop, all parts of the soul are affected by sin. Goodwin speaks of sin's total defilement: "It rests not in one member only, but beginning at the understanding, eats into the will and affections, soaks through all. Those diseases we account strongest, which seize not on a joint or member only, but strike rottenness through the whole body."[21] Sin's contagion spreads not only from Adam to his posterity but everywhere within each person.

John Murray (1898–1975), referring to Genesis 6:5 and 8:21, made several appropriate comments with regards to sin's contagion:

"There is the *intensity*—'The wickedness of man was great in the earth'; there is the *inwardness*—'the imagination of the thoughts of his heart', an expression unsurpassed in the usage of Scripture to indicate that the most rudimentary movement of thought was evil; there is the *totality*—'every imagination'; there is the *constancy*—'continually'; there is the *exclusiveness*—'only evil'; there is the *early manifestation*—'from his youth.'"[22] Although we are not as bad as we could be due to God's restraining grace, we sin with intensity in an exclusively evil manner and that from birth. Sin has diffused itself to reach every part of man's being, body and soul: "The whole head is sick, and the whole heart faint" (Isa. 1:5).

The Canons of Dort (1618–19) offer brief but penetrating insight into the doctrine of human depravity. The loss of holiness, in which we possessed "a true and sound knowledge of the Creator and things spiritual, in will and heart with righteousness, and in all emotions with purity," robbed us of these "outstanding gifts."[23] Instead, our depravity consists in "blindness, terrible darkness, futility, and distortion of judgment in [our] minds; perversity, defiance, and hardness in [our] hearts and wills; and finally impurity in all [our] emotions."[24] Corrupt children bring forth the same. Since, by nature, we are born children of wrath, "all people are conceived in sin and are born children of wrath, unfit for any saving good, inclined to evil, dead in their sins, and slaves to sin."[25] Thus total depravity also includes "total inability" (i.e., we are unable to create spiritual life in ourselves). It is wrongheaded to suggest therefore that Christians are totally depraved. Once God sovereignly works spiritual life into us through the work of the Spirit uniting us to Christ, Christians are no longer "totally depraved." They now possess the ability to respond to God with acts of faith, hope, and love.

Since we cannot produce spiritual life in ourselves, nothing truly good and praiseworthy can proceed from an unregenerate nature. A bad tree brings forth bad fruit (Matt. 7:17–18). In ourselves, we are *not able* to *not sin*. The doctrine of total depravity is bad news for people, and few enjoy receiving bad news, especially when we hear that our perceived good is evil according to God's righteous standards. Notwithstanding, the outward good often done by unbelievers is, to borrow from Augustine, an example of "splendid vices." In a sense, we can recognize the "good job" of unbelievers contributing to the common good of mankind by the common grace of God at work in the entire world. But, in the end, every work of the unbeliever gets performed without faith in Christ, through the power of the Spirit, and for His glory. In this sense, no work of an unbeliever qualifies as a truly good work.

This natural depravity does not deny the free will of unbelievers, but only claims that those without Christ possess no willing inclination to do that which is truly good. Sadly, their wills incline naturally toward evil. Sin also occurs in the intellect, since deliberation to sin is usually the first step in the committing of actual sins proceeding from original sin. Because the mind as well as the soul is affected by original sin, the will has a certain propensity toward evil.

APPLICATION

The moment we enter this world we stand guilty before a holy God and face His eternal judgment in hell, unless He shows grace to us and grants us salvation. Our natural sinful hearts are mini hells; they are places where the devil is enthroned without any rival until Christ comes and dethrones him. Here then, in this seemingly hopeless narrative, there exists hope in Christ.

In a sense, Adam, as representative of humanity, put off the "new self" and put on the "old self" (Eph. 4:22–24). Jesus is the "new man," the visible image of God. In Christ we can put on the "new self" again. Paul challenges you to "put off your old self," the way you used to live in your pursuit of pleasure and things of this world. Now, in Christ, informed and transformed by the truths of Scripture and the power of the Spirit, he wants you "to put on the new self," and run from the things you know are sinful while striving to do good according to the commands of God. What we lost we can get back in Christ, and, as a result of it coming from Him, we get it better than Adam ever had it even before he sinned.

Original sin meant we incurred guilt, pollution, and a loss of sonship. But in Christ we receive benefits from Him and in Him that answer to these ills: justification, sanctification, and adoption.

3

SIN'S PRIVATION: YOU'VE LOST THAT LOVIN' FEELING

SIN'S ESSENCE

We may have an idea of what sin does: it is the soul's disease, blinding the mind, hardening the heart, disordering the will, stealing strength, and dampening the affections.

But what is sin? How we define sin reveals a lot about our understanding of it. We err by focusing too much on actual sins and neglecting the fact that sin, always against God, involves not just actions but also inclinations and desires that may or may not lead to an act.

Some have wrongly thought of sin as an alien substance that enters our being and defiles us. Sin indeed inhabits and infects every one of us. But sin is not of the essence of human nature and is not a substance. What is it, then? What does it mean to sin? Are we responsible for all of our inclinations? Are our inclinations voluntary or not? These questions are crucial for understanding both ourselves and our relation to God—not only as sinners but also as saints.

PRIVATION AND POSITIVE INCLINATION

In defining sin, we may distinguish between two parts: privation, or the absence of a quality normally present; and positive inclination, or the tendency to commit evil. Privation (Latin: *privatio*) is used in contrast to the idea of sin's substantiality, but sometimes one finds the concept of "actual privation" to highlight the activeness of sin. Going back to Augustine, privation denotes the loss of original righteousness. This absence of good should not be understood as "mere privation," though it involves an incomplete privation (as opposed to a complete privation), since sin does not entirely abolish the human will. In other words, we are not destitute of any semblance of God's image, which would be "complete privation." And "mere privation" would miss the concept of "positive inclination," which was always coupled with "privation." When Reformed theologians speak of "positive inclination" they are not speaking in an ethical sense, as if sin were positively good. Nor are they speaking of positive inclination in a physical sense (then it would also be good since created by God). Instead, by "positive" they mean it in a logical sense, that is, it is asserted about man that he does such and such (e.g., "evil continually," Gen. 6:5).

Goodwin says that sin is, first, a "total and utter emptiness and privation of all that righteousness and true holiness which God first created in man, and which the law of God requires. And, *second*, a positive sinful inclination to all that is contrary to grace, namely, a proneness to all sin, of what kind soever, which any law of God forbids; which positive sinfulness is divided into two parts."[1] According to Goodwin, these two parts include:

(1) The inordinate lustings of the faculties after things earthly, fleshly, sinful;
(2) An enmity unto God, and unto what is holy.[2]

Basically, sin involves not only the lack of righteousness but also the inclination toward unrighteousness, which always leads to enmity against a holy, righteous, infinitely good God. On the flip side, the biblical Christian ethic of holiness understands that true righteousness, the opposite of sin, involves not only refraining from evil but doing good (Eph. 4:25–29).

Sin is the inclination, which may be an action (e.g., lying) or a non-action (e.g., failing to speak the truth), against God's law. Bavinck's own description of sin is noteworthy: "Sin, accordingly, has to be understood and described neither as an existing thing nor as being in things that exist but rather as a defect, a deprivation, an absence of the good, as weakness, imbalance, just as blindness is a deprivation of sight."[3] Burroughs also speaks of sin's evil as nothingness: "All things that have a being, there is some good in them; for God hath a Being, and every thing that hath a being hath some good in it, because it is of God; but Sin is a Non Entity, a no being: [It is] rather the deprivation of a Being than any being at all. [And] here is a great mystery of Iniquity, That that which is a Non-entity in it self, yet should have such a mighty efficacy to trouble heaven and earth."[4] How remarkable that a "non-entity" should be so powerful.

Sin is a parasite of the good; it feeds off of what God created. It manipulates that which is good and distorts, perverts, defaces, and spoils it. So, privation as a lack of righteousness provides only half of the story when it comes to understanding sin. As we are not neutral beings, we must also take account of our positive inclination toward rebellion against God and man. This destructive power in us leads to the various descriptions we have seen for sin (e.g., unrighteousness, transgression, lawlessness).

For sin to be a material or spiritual substance, one of two things must be true: God would have to be its cause, or He would have to be the creator of all things except for sin. Both of these are impossible. Sin's nature is, therefore, understood as an ethical problem, not a physical problem.[5] Resulting from a disordered will that moves away from God, sin is privation but not negation. That a fish does not speak is a negation; that a human does not speak is a privation since, ordinarily, a human is made to speak. Sin is therefore the privation of the righteousness a human ought to have as one made in the image of God.

Even though we speak of sin as privation, we can also speak of it as an "action." Think of a man with a broken leg trying to make his way to the hospital after a terrible accident. His walking is "walking" (an action), but it is a malfunctioning, defective walk. Relating this concrete image to sin, the man actually walks in a deformed manner toward his executioner rather than toward his healer at the hospital since sin draws us away from good.

In Romans 5:6–9, Paul highlights our privation, our weakness, as well as our positive inclination toward unrighteousness. In our natural state we are called "weak" and "ungodly" (v. 6). Christ died for "sinners" (v. 8) who were "enemies" (v. 9) of God. Here we see both the privative and the positive part of our sinfulness. We are "weak" or powerless, in contrast to Christ's resurrection power (Rom. 1:4). We naturally possess moral frailty. From a physical perspective, imagine the horrendous scene of a person with terminal cancer lying on a bed ready to die. There is no power to live. We lack such health spiritually; we are living but not really living (1 Thess. 3:8).

But we are by nature also godless. The wicked of the unredeemed world are earlier described by Paul in Romans as ungodly (1:18; 4:5). They are those who not only lack righteousness but also replace it with wickedness (Rom. 1:21–31). We are estranged from God and His life of grace, which leaves us spiritually impotent. To be godly is to have the life of God in our souls, to be filled with the goodness that comes from above. Ungodliness is the destitute state of the person without God and without hope (Eph. 2:12).

Those who are spiritually impotent, lacking the power of God, are then only what they can be: sinners (Rom. 5:8). Privation leads to sin, which is corrupting; it is not idle but energetic. The due righteousness is replaced by unrighteousness; the absence of what is good is replaced by the corruption of our disposition that properly leads to our designation as sinners.

As sinners we are naturally enemies of God, since all sin is ultimately against God. Sin leads us astray from God, and at the same time places us against Him, which makes us His enemies. Paul speaks of the godless sinners apart from Christ as those "who once were alienated and hostile in mind, doing evil deeds" (Col. 1:21).

Regarding sins of omission and commission, the twofold nature of sin holds up. Sins of omission concern those affirming what each commandment requires. So, the command to not kill demands the preservation of life. Failure to lawfully maintain life (e.g., stopping to assist at a car accident), so far as we are able, is a privation of the righteous requirements of the law. Sins of commission relate to our positive inclinations toward unrighteousness in doing what is forbidden. The privation of omission is deadly to our souls because we are bound to act a certain way in various circumstances, but we fail to be who we were created to be. What is worse, we replace what is owed to God with what is forbidden by God in our committing the opposite of what is commanded. Original sin, which infects us as we are created in the womb, is therefore against the law of God because there is a privation of original righteousness that is required by the law of God. This, as will be noted later, has implications for sins that do not fully terminate as actual sins, but reside only in the mind.

ETHICAL AND SPIRITUAL IMPLICATIONS

Lacking its own independent existence as a substance, sin is an ethical opposite to what is good. Sin needed the good for its expression, for it only exists by and in connection and contrast with the good. Satan was a holy angel before he became evil. Adam was created in holiness and righteousness before sin marred his original constitution. Sin borrows from the good, not from some independent evil that exists apart from God's creation. Sin does not so obliterate our humanity in the image of God that we no longer now have a will, feelings, or passions. Adam had a will and passions before his fall, and nothing fundamentally changed in terms of the possession of these characteristics. Rather, the form of these characteristics was distorted and perverted. Adam did not stop loving or desiring; but his love and desire in his fallen estate was disordered. As Bavinck says, "Substantially, sin has neither removed anything from humanity nor introduced anything into it. It is the same human person, but now walking, not toward God but away from him, to destruction."[6]

Since sin is ethical, what determines the rightness or wrongness of an action must be in relation to God's being and His law. The "splendid vices" of unbelievers are actions that can, in a sense, be called virtues. Depending on the motive and context, those outside of Christ can and do practice outwardly virtuous acts that, by all accounts, reflect the law of God and occur in His common grace to all humanity. But, as we dig a little more, the law of God is not merely some outward form that exists as a standard of righteousness. The law is divine, coming from God Himself. Outward virtues are not the same thing as good works, which must be done in faith, by the Spirit, to the glory of God. The law of God, implanted in the human heart at creation, was also delivered at Mount Sinai, and remains a rule for Christians in their state of grace (Rom. 13:8–10). Good works must satisfy the demands of the law as spiritual.

VOLUNTARY AND INVOLUNTARY SIN

Only beings with a created will can be guilty of sin against God's law. God has endowed humans alone with a will, as rational creatures. The will always acts in relation to the moral law, either in obedience or disobedience to its demands. But sins of ignorance and concupiscence, while lesser in degree of their sinfulness, are not thereby excluded or excused. Impure desires that arise in our understanding apart from a direct act of the will are still sin.

We can understand sin as voluntary by a distinction between the will considered narrowly (strictly) or broadly (generally). Narrowly speaking, it refers to that which is done by a movement of the will. Broadly speaking, however, it refers to anything that effects the will or depends upon it. All sin is voluntary if we speak broadly. But, narrowly, not all sin is necessarily voluntary. That does not mean that a certain sin could bypass the will. The act of the will may lead to actual sins, but sin may occur prior to the acting of the will. Unclean thoughts, for example, may not lead to acts but to say they are not sin goes against the consistent teaching of the Reformed tradition and indeed of all Protestants. Some in the Roman Catholic tradition had argued that involuntary motions opposed to God's law are not sins.

Francis Turretin makes the point that the "very first motions of concupiscence do not cease to be sins, although they are neither wholly voluntary nor in our power" (Rom. 7:7).[7] Returning to the will considered broadly, Bavinck explains how involuntary sins simply cannot occur apart from the human will: "There is not only an antecedent but also a concomitant, a consequent, and an approving will. Later, to a greater or lesser degree, the will approves of the sinfulness of our nature and takes delight in it . . . even the sin that is done without having been willed does not occur totally apart from the will."[8] All of this is to say, we can never excuse our unclean thoughts or desires just because they are not voluntary acts. The will, in a certain sense, is always at work since as humans we are never not willing. Hence, sin has its degrees (see James 1:14–15).

Commenting on James 4:16, Thomas Manton (1620–77) says, "First we practice sin, then defend it, then boast of it. Sin is first our burden, then our custom, then our delight, then our excellency."[9] A little more precisely, we may speak of the degrees of sin in this way:

1. The deliberation to sin, which is an act of the will (broadly speaking).
2. The decision to commit an actual sin.
3. The act of sinning, which has in view voluntary sins as an act of the will (narrowly speaking).
4. A pleasure in the act of sinning, which increases the heinousness of the sin.
5. Boasting after the act, which is the opposite of repentance.

The first degree of sin, which is not as heinous as the following degrees, occurs in the intellect, which, as we have said, is not apart (broadly speaking) from the human will. In inward temptation, the enticing desire (Greek: *epithymia*) is sin, as James notes (1:14–15). It is a violation of the tenth commandment, "You shall not covet..." (Ex. 20:17; see also Rom. 7:7–13). The deliberation to sin, understood as a disordered desire, cannot be excused even if it is not formally acted upon. It may be a lesser sin than if it had been acted upon and even subsequently enjoyed; but it is still sin because we are ultimately fully responsible for the inner workings of our heart, soul, mind, and strength. Thankfully, by the Spirit (Rom. 8:13), we have the power to take our thoughts captive in obedience to Christ (2 Cor. 10:5). Conscious that we can inwardly be sinfully tempted, we depend upon God to change the inner man so that we can have the mind of Christ (1 Cor. 2:16), and so, by God's grace, desire less and less things that are contrary to His will. In addition, while we do not excuse our disordered thoughts, we praise God that He keeps us from acting out on so much of what goes on inside. These are all mercies.

HUMAN ACTIONS

As we act as human beings, we should remember that our actings are not usually evil. Our rational faculties are, as we have seen, not lost from our state of innocence. For example, just as Adam was made to eat and breathe, so we eat and breathe. Adam would not, however, have eaten to the point of being gluttonous. Reformed theologians have even argued that all actions are good in terms of their physical goodness, whether an act of the mind or the body. But not all actions are morally good. There is a distinction then between a physical goodness and a moral goodness. Looking with the eyes is good, but looking to lust is bad. As Charnock says, "The physical goodness of the action depends on God, the moral evil on the creature."[10] An action of killing may be either good or bad, depending upon the circumstances. The physical action is not bad per se, but the moral goodness of the action depends, as Charnock says, upon the "objects, circumstances, and constitution of the mind in the doing of it."[11]

God designed us to worship, which involves the whole person (Deut. 6:4–6). Physically, the act of worship is neutral, such as bowing down or falling down (Ex. 24:1; Acts 10:25). In worship we also apply our minds and hearts to God. But if we worship anything other than God, whether a false god or a statue in place of Him, we have committed a moral evil. The same is true for our language. The act of speaking is a physical good, a gift from the God who speaks and makes us to be like Him. But the tongue may also be an instrument of evil. As James says, "With it we bless our Lord and Father, and with it we curse people who are made in the likeness of God" (3:9). The physical motions that produce words are good, but the moral goodness of the act depends upon what is said and the integrity of the words spoken (i.e., from a pure heart).

We return then to our definition of sin in terms of our actions. The sinfulness of our actions consists, says Charnock, "in a privation of that . . . righteousness which ought to be in an action, in a want of conformity of the act with the law of God. . . . Now the sinfulness of an action is not the act itself, but is considered in it as it is related to the law, and is a deviation from it; and so it is something cleaving to the action, and therefore to be distinguished from the act itself, which is the subject of the sinfulness."[12] To call an action sinful we mean, adds Charnock, that "the action is the subject, and the sinfulness of the action is that which adheres to it. The action is not the sinfulness, nor the sinfulness the action; they are distinguished, as the member and a disease in the member, the arm and the palsy in it. The arm is not the palsy, nor is the palsy the arm; but the palsy is a disease that cleaves to the arm. So sinfulness is a deformity that cleaves to an action."[13]

This is reminiscent of Augustine's famous sermon on love from 1 John 4:4–12 where he says the root of love determines the Christian's actions:

> A father [spanks] a boy, while a kidnapper caresses him. Offered a choice between blows and caresses, who would not choose the caresses and avoid the blows? But when you consider the people who give them you realize that it is love that [spanks], wickedness that caresses. This is what I insist upon: human actions can only be understood by their root in love. All kinds of actions might appear good without proceeding from the root of love. Remember, thorns also have flowers: some actions seem truly savage, but are done for the sake of discipline motivated by love. Once and for all, I give you this one short command: love God, and do what you will.[14]

The doing of an action is not the problem, but the root of the doing. Of course, it must be in obedience to the law, since sin is an ethical–spiritual matter. But, as Paul says, "If I give away all I have, and if I deliver up my body to be burned, but have not love, I gain nothing" (1 Cor. 13:3).

APPLICATION

Sin is a mystery that we cannot understand but that we must acknowledge. Bavinck's words are moving yet terrifying:

> We know neither whence it is nor what it is. It exists, but has no right to existence. It exists but no one can explain its origin. Sin itself came into the world without motivation, yet it is the motivation for all human thought and actions. From an abstract point of view, it is nothing but a privation, yet concretely it is a power that controls everyone and everything. It has no independent principle of its own, yet it is a principle that devastates the whole creation. It lives off the good, yet fights it to the point of destruction. It is nothing, has nothing, and cannot do anything without the entities and forces God has created, yet organizes them all into rebellion against him.... It is the greatest contradiction tolerated by God in his creation, yet used by him in the way of justice and righteousness as an instrument for his glory.[15]

After all, God uses the devil against himself; in his implacable hatred toward Christ, he sought to have Him killed and yet it was Christ's death that defeated Satan. God somehow, in His infinite wisdom, uses sin for His glory and very often our good.

We may not know what sin is, but we do understand something of its nature and effects upon us. We know that sin has a twofold effect upon us: it robs us of righteousness and holiness, and it explains our proneness to evil. For example, we have excessive and lustful desires for pleasure and often in connection with a rebellious hardness to God and His ways. As we run to sin, we run from God; as we run from God we run to sin.

What's more, we are never guiltless for our thoughts and actions that are contrary to God's law. Even those motions of the heart and mind that do not erupt into actual sins are nevertheless sins. What does this all mean? We need to reckon with this formidable foe. One can remember Luther's saying about faith: "O it is a living, busy, active, mighty thing, this faith."[16] Sin, we may say too, is a busy, active, mighty thing, and those who do not see it as an enemy will be destroyed by it. When we understand that we have no answer in ourselves to sin, then we are in the position to go to the only One who can deal with this problem: The God and Father of our Lord Jesus Christ.

4

SIN'S VOCABULARY: FADE TO BLACK

DEFINITIONS

After David committed adultery with Bathsheba and consequently plotted the death of Uriah, he languished with a false peace that required Nathan the prophet to finally confront him with his sin. The result was Psalm 51, a masterpiece of penitential literature and one superintended by the Holy Spirit. There, David does not merely say he has sinned, though he does of course say that (v. 4). Rather, his repentance prompts him to mine deeply the biblical vocabulary for sin, offering us a more acute picture of the heinousness of his actions that involved carnally knowing a woman not his wife and murdering a man not his enemy. In the Psalm, David speaks of "my transgressions" (vv. 1, 3), "my iniquity" (vv. 2, 9b), "my sin" (v. 3), doing "evil" (v. 4), being "brought forth in iniquity" (v. 5a), being conceived "in sin" (v. 5b), "my sins" (v. 9a), and "bloodguiltiness" (v. 14). In other words, it did not suffice for David to simply say he "missed the mark."

To merely describe sin as "missing the mark" is a gross injustice to the actual vocabulary of the Bible and the nature of sin. Even our catechetical instruction on sin can leave us with an underdeveloped doctrine of sin if we do not dig deeper into the biblical picture. After all, sin defined as "any want of conformity unto, or transgression of, the law of God" (Westminster Shorter Catechism, A. 14) needs further unpacking. Indeed, as sinners we fail to conform to God's righteous standards: "Everyone who makes a practice of sinning also practices lawlessness; sin is lawlessness" (1 John 3:4). Also, we not only fail to do what God commands, but we also rebelliously pursue what He prohibits: "For the mind that is set on the flesh is hostile to God, for it does not submit to God's law; indeed, it cannot" (Rom. 8:7).

Understanding the wide-ranging assortment of the biblical descriptions of sin offers us a clearer view of the appalling character of sin. This makes sense theologically insofar as God names and describes Himself at different times in redemptive history as a way for us to know His character. Crucial in any discussion on the nature of sin is the undisputed biblical fact that sin is directly against a holy, righteous, unchangeably good God (Ps. 51:4). Sin is theocentric (Rom. 1:18–32), and thus illegal (Rom. 3:20). In this sense, it is anti-relational as we, the offenders, rise up in enmity against God, the offended.[1] When we hate God, we as fellow image-bearers stand no chance in our natural disposition toward one another. The vocabulary of sin in the Scriptures is designed to help us understand what sin is and why it is a problem.

OLD TESTAMENT

The importance of the Old Testament teaching on sin includes the plethora of words used to describe sin, as well as the many different manifestations of sin in the lives of the godly and the wicked. We get a fascinating look at the peculiarities of the human personality in the vividly portrayed stories of individuals, groups, and nations. The book of Genesis, for example, explores human nature in ways that are deeply profound, such as that tricky character called Jacob who needed a lot of work (and patience) from above. David, Absalom, and Manasseh provide fascinating looks into the peculiar character of sin and its consequences. As enlightening as studies on various characters may be, something needs to be said about the precise language God uses in His Word for sin.

The Hebrew root, *hātā*, generally refers to the idea of erring, doing wrong, missing the mark, or going astray, which may or may not relate directly to sin. Still, the word is the most common for sin in the Old Testament. Sometimes physical language even symbolizes the same spiritually in that passage. For example, in Proverbs 19:2 the English translates as "missing the way": "Desire without knowledge is not good, and whoever makes haste with his feet misses his way." But of course, the straying here is understood spiritually in terms of impetuosity. The hasty person sinfully "rushes into things" by acting without thinking, which is a form of pride. Pride is at odds with patient waiting on the Lord. As we can see, we have to be careful with word studies, making sure to do them with the context in mind. Here, in the wisdom literature of Proverbs, the term denotes sin in terms of an everyday experience symbolic of a moral failure.

The verb "rebel" (*pāšā'*) refers to willful rebellion either against God or other humans. So Israel "rebelled against" God (Ezek. 2:3) and, on a human level, "against the house of David to this day" (1 Kings 12:19; see also 2 Kings 1:1). Closely connected to this verb is *sārâ*, whose root refers generally to departure from a path and can denote a spiritual and stubborn deviation from such: "Why will you still be struck down? Why will you continue to rebel?" (Isa. 1:5; see also Deut. 13:5).

The noun *ma'al* refers to treachery or faithlessness: "And I will make the land desolate, because they have acted faithlessly, declares the Lord GOD" (Ezek. 15:8); "I will spread my net over him, and he shall be taken in my snare, and I will bring him to Babylon and enter into judgment with him there for the treachery he has committed against me" (Ezek. 17:20). Abomination (*tô'ēbâ*) is also used to describe something repulsive, which may refer to something God abhors or even something that people abhor. One may sacrifice a blemished sheep, for example, and this would be an abomination to God (Deut. 17:1); or sexual perversions, such as a man lying with another man, may be called an abomination (Lev. 18:22). The term 'ārar, which denotes a curse, frequently appears in the curse formulas as a specific and formal declaration of punishment (Gen. 3:14, 17), often with a threatening aspect (Jer. 11:3).

Various other Old Testament words occur for sin, depending on the specific English translation: mischief, wickedness, trouble, wrong, error, fraud, crime, etc. The Old Testament term often translated as "iniquity" ('awôn) is particularly illuminating. Based upon its frequent usage (more than two hundred instances), we come to the conclusion that it refers in the first place to the iniquitous act itself; second, to the guilt that accompanies all iniquitous acts; and, third, to the inevitable punishment that must result from the act of iniquity. The suffering servant in Isaiah 53 bears our iniquities (vv. 6, 11).

In Exodus 34:6–7, the Lord proclaims that He is "merciful and gracious, slow to anger, and abounding in steadfast love and faithfulness, keeping steadfast love for thousands, forgiving iniquity and transgression and sin, but who will by no means clear the guilty, visiting the iniquity of the fathers on the children and the children's children, to the third and the fourth generation." In one of the most glorious revelations of His attributes, we also have one of the fiercest declarations of God's wrath upon those whose fathers have committed iniquity. Here we are faced with the danger of iniquity. It is not an individual problem, but a corporate one (e.g., racism). Just as righteous parents bring many blessings to their children, it is also true that children suffer for the sins of their parents. An ominous example of corporate punishment for iniquity occurs in 1 Samuel 3:13–14. The house of Eli is punished forever, "for the iniquity that he knew, because his sons were blaspheming God, and he did not restrain them. Therefore I swear to the house of Eli that the iniquity of Eli's house shall not be atoned for by sacrifice or offering forever." Eli did not restrain his wicked sons, and so his household suffered as a consequence. Sin left unchecked will lead to ruinous consequences.

The Old Testament also speaks regularly of the wicked (*rāšā'*). The adjective *rāšā'* is the most frequently used term to described wicked persons, often in contrast to the righteous (e.g., Gen. 18:23, "Will you indeed sweep away the righteous with the wicked?"; Ps. 1:6, "for the LORD knows the way of the righteous, but the way of the wicked will perish"). The wicked offer evil counsel (Ps. 1:1) and in Psalm 10 we are told that the wicked person pursues the poor (v. 2), curses and renounces the Lord (v. 3), lives as a practical atheist (v. 4), deceives and oppresses (v. 7), speaks "mischief and iniquity" (v. 7), seizes the poor (v. 9), and believes God will not remember his actions (v. 11). Wickedness invariably leads to practical atheism. As such, God will vindicate the righteous and destroy the unrepentant wicked (Ps. 1:4–6). So, unless the wicked listen to God's prophets who call upon them to repent and turn from their wicked ways toward God:

> "Let the wicked forsake his way,
>   and the unrighteous man his thoughts;
> let him return to the LORD, that he may have compassion
>   on him,
>   and to our God, for he will abundantly pardon." (Isa. 55:7)

The way away from God, for someone who should know better, is indeed wicked. But even for the wicked we see the amazing compassion of God who does not only pardon, but abundantly pardons. Again, so often we see in God's Word that right next to God's condemnation of the sinner we find a testimony to God's grace to the same.

NEW TESTAMENT

In the New Testament we often read the words "sin," "commit sin," "sinful," and "sinner." Paul uses these words almost one hundred times with sixty of them in the book of Romans. "Missing the mark," in the sense of reducing sin to a mere mistake (as in responding to moral rebellion with "to err is human"), dilutes its rebellion against and deviation from God's law.

The verb "to sin" (*hamartanō*) occurs frequently in the New Testament, either referring to a specific act or a force with power (Rom. 5:21). Sinful behavior can be used to describe a group of people: "And the scribes of the Pharisees, when they saw that he was eating with sinners and tax collectors . . . " (Mark 2:16); "but God shows his love for us in that while we were still sinners, Christ died for us" (Rom. 5:8).

Sin can be understood also by the use of other terms such as "flesh" (*sarx*). The term can refer to physical flesh ("they did not find the body of the Lord Jesus," Luke 24:3), the physical constitution of human nature ("Blessed are you, Simon Bar-Jonah! For flesh and blood has not revealed this to you," Matt. 16:17), and blood relationships ("my brothers, my kinsmen according to the flesh," Rom. 9:3). There is also the obvious sense in which "the flesh" is subjected to weakness ("the spirit indeed is willing, but the flesh is weak," Matt. 26:41). The Pauline usage of *sarx* very often refers to sinful nature ("For I know that nothing good dwells in me, that is, in my flesh," Rom. 7:18; "For if you live according to the flesh you will die," Rom. 8:13). The Christian experiences a daily struggle between the (sinful) flesh and the Spirit; the desires of both are contrary. Paul lists "sexual immorality, impurity, sensuality, idolatry, sorcery, enmity, strife, jealousy, fits of anger, rivalries, dissensions, divisions, envy, drunkenness, orgies, and things like these," as works of the flesh (Gal. 5:19–21). These need to be mortified (Rom. 8:13), or we will not inherit the kingdom of God (Gal. 5:21).

Other words appear as well, giving a fuller picture of the biblical vocabulary for sin. Lawlessness (*anomía*) appears in Matthew 23:28 as Jesus describes the scribes and Pharisees: "So you also outwardly appear righteous to others, but within you are full of hypocrisy and lawlessness." To the surprise of some, the Pharisees (and chief priests) were lawless. God's law is the standard for right and wrong. All sin must be a transgression of God's law. We have our knowledge of sin because of God's law (Rom. 3:20; 7:7). Thus Jesus asked the lawless Pharisees, "And why do you break the commandment of God for the sake of your tradition?" (Matt. 15:3). He then proceeded in the following verses (vv. 4–7) to expose them for breaking the fifth commandment. Moreover, they broke the first and second commandments because they rejected the purpose of God by refusing John's baptism (Luke 7:30); the fourth commandment by failing to do good on the Sabbath (Matt. 12:9–14; Luke 6:9–11); the sixth commandment, as they sought to kill our Lord ("Has not Moses given you the law? Yet none of you keeps the law. Why do you seek to kill me?" John 7:19); the eighth commandment as they devoured widows' houses (Mark 12:40); the ninth commandment with lying ("Tell people, 'His disciples came by night and stole him away while we were asleep,'" Matt. 28:13); and the tenth commandment in coveting ("Pharisees, who were lovers of money," Luke 16:14).

The Greek word *adikia*, translated variously as "injustice," "unrighteousness," "evil," or "iniquity," occurs frequently throughout the New Testament (e.g., Rom. 1:18, 29; 2:8; 3:5; 6:13; 9:14; Luke 13:27; 16:9; 18:6). This unrighteousness that characterizes humanity in sin is only unrighteousness because of a righteous God, against whom sin ultimately occurs. Our transgressions against the law are proof of our unrighteousness. Those who break the law or cross a boundary have committed a transgression (*parabasis*) (Rom. 4:15b). The law was added because of transgressions (Gal. 3:19). Eve was deceived and "became a transgressor" (1 Tim. 2:14). Similarly, Adam is accused of a trespass (*paraptōma*) (Rom. 5:20), which carries the idea of a violation or moral failure.

From a rich Old Testament foundation, the New Testament also employs the word "unclean" ("impurity"), to emphasize man's sin and waywardness preventing him from being holy and near to the Holy One. Paul speaks of the pagan Gentiles, who gave "themselves up to sensuality, greedy to practice every kind of impurity" (Eph. 4:19). He thus warns Christians that "sexual immorality and all impurity or covetousness must not even be named among you, as is proper among saints" (Eph. 5:3). One of the greatest judgments of God upon humanity is when He gives people over "in the lusts of their hearts to impurity" (Rom. 1:24).

The book of Jude is a passionate polemic against ungodly teachers who pervert the grace of our God into sensuality (v. 4), thus denying God in unfaithfulness. The Lord will come and "convict all the ungodly of all their deeds of ungodliness that they have committed in such an ungodly way" (v. 15). Of what does their ungodliness consist? They are "grumblers, malcontents, following their own sinful desires; they are loud-mouthed boasters, showing favoritism to gain advantage" (v. 16). This "sensuality" (v. 4) can also refer to a type of "self-abandonment" shown in a lack of control over oneself. Those active on social media should be able to testify to the reality of these sins. Occurring ten times in the New Testament, this sin often denotes sins of a sexual nature (Rom. 13:13; 2 Peter 2:7). Such are linked to the sin of debauchery (*asōtia*), which is also a form of uncontrolled living according to one's sinful passions (1 Peter 4:4).

Paul presents a rather complex view of the law, but in line with promoting its goodness (Rom. 7:16) when used lawfully (1 Tim. 1:8). Still, in 1 Timothy 1:9–10 he explains that the law is not given for the righteous but the "lawless and disobedient" (v. 9). He then uses various words to describe how such lawless people relate to specific commandments:

first commandment: "ungodly" (v. 9) ("You shall have no other gods before me," Ex. 20:3).

second commandment: "sinners" (v. 9) (A possible reference to Gentile idolatry).

third commandment: "profane" (v. 9) ("You shall not take the name of the LORD your God in vain . . ." Ex. 20:7).

fourth commandment: "unholy" (v. 9) ("Remember the Sabbath day, to keep it holy," Ex. 20:8).

fifth commandment: "strike their fathers and mothers" (v. 9) ("Honor your father and your mother," Ex. 20:12).

sixth commandment: "murderers" (v. 9) ("You shall not murder," Ex. 20:13).

seventh commandment: "sexually immoral" (v. 10) / "men who practice homosexuality" (v. 10) ("You shall not commit adultery," Ex. 20:14).

eighth commandment: "enslavers" (v. 10) ("You shall not steal," Ex. 20:15).

ninth commandment: "liars, perjurers" (v. 10) ("You shall not bear false witness against your neighbor," Ex. 20:16).

APPLICATION

The vivid description of sinners reveals an important biblical point that we sometimes overlook in our thinking; namely, we are more than "mere sinners." It is one thing to simply say people are "sinners," but the Scriptures offer a rich vocabulary of sin. We find words such as "transgression," "debauchery," or "iniquity." A murderer is a transgressor or one who commits iniquity. In a legal setting, a criminal does not simply say, "I sinned, but we are all sinners." If guilty, he has to own up to the specific sin and sometimes a unique word or phrase is offered to highlight the severity of the crime.

We can say we are all sinners (Rom. 3:23), but we capture

something slightly different when we speak of homosexual activity as an unnatural abomination before God (Rom. 1:27; Lev. 18:22). We may see pagan debauchery taking place and we say "they are sinning" or we could say it is "lawlessness," which helps us to explicitly focus on the fact that a law (God's law) is being broken. Similarly, rape is vile and contemptuous, a violation of another's dignity in the extremity. A person is seized, assaulted, humiliated, and suffers a loss of dignity because of the violation (Deut. 22:28–29). Yes, it is a sin; but God offers language that helps to understand the nature of the crime. All sins are bad, but not all sins are equally bad (John 19:11). All sins are sin but not all sins are the same sin.

With this in mind, just as there is a rich vocabulary for sin, there is an even richer one for grace. Returning to Psalm 51, we see this in David's hope. If sin is as bad as David confesses, salvation from sin must be greater. Thus, David speaks of God's "steadfast love" and "abundant mercy" (v. 1). He asks to be washed and cleansed (v. 2); he asks to be "purged" in order to be clean, to be washed in order to be whiter than snow (v. 7). God is the one who "blots out" and hides His face from our sins (v. 9). He creates clean hearts and renews right spirits within the repentant (v. 10); He gives us the Spirit (v. 11) and restores the joy of salvation (v. 12). The One who delivers us from bloodguiltiness (v. 14) is the One who also establishes our praise and accepts our worship (vv. 14–17). Sin is bad, very bad; but God is good, very good.

5

SIN'S REMAINS: HELLO DARKNESS, MY OLD FRIEND

WORSE THAN POISON

Thomas Watson says, "While we carry the fire of sin about us, we must carry the waters of tears to quench it."[1] As long as we live we shall be repenting, because we will be sinning.

A true awareness of who we are by nature occurs through the work of the Holy Spirit. Watson puts it provocatively when he says, "Sin makes a man worse than a toad or serpent. The serpent has nothing but what God has put into it. Poison is medicinable [i.e., it has a use as medicine]; but the sinner has that which the devil has put into him."[2] With conversion, the guilt of sin is eradicated, and the dominion of sin broken, yet the remainders of sin abide in believers. Welcome to the doctrine of Indwelling Sin.

Few believers attempt to deny the presence of sin in them after conversion. Some have vainly imagined they can attain or come close to perfection in this life, but such a view is hardly worth addressing given the clear teaching of Scripture on this matter (1 John 1:8). The real matter for consideration is the nature, power, and effects of sin that remain in believers after they have been born again into a living hope (1 Peter 1:3, 23). With John Haydon (*d.* 1782), we can refer to indwelling sin as the "unhappy experience of all good men, while they continue in this world."[3]

The Puritan Samuel Bolton (c. 1606–54) puts it well in *The True Bounds of Christian Freedom*:

> Though still we have the presence; nay, the stirrings and working of corruptions, which makes us to have many a sad heart and wet eye. Yet Christ has thus far freed us from sin; it shall not have dominion. There may be the turbulence, but not the prevalence of sin. . . . It was said of Carthage that Rome was more troubled with it when half destroyed than when whole. So a godly man may be more troubled with sin when it is conquered than when it reigned.[4]

We are now more troubled by sin than when we were formerly living in darkness. Now we see its horrors, mainly because we have our eyes opened to the glorious God, against whom sin is committed.

TWO TYPES OF LAWS

There has been and continues to be some lively debate over the meaning of Paul's language concerning his struggle with sin in Romans 7. Among the most well-known views, the two that are most prevalent concern whether Paul speaks as a Christian or as someone not yet in Christ. The arguments on both sides are compelling, but Paul seems to speak in a way that no unconverted person could. He speaks in a way that many Christians instinctively recognize as true in their own battle with sin.

C. E. B. Cranfield (1915–2015) argues:

> Verse 25b is an embarrassment to those who see in v. 24 the cry of an unconverted man or of a Christian living on a low level of Christian life and in v. 25a an indication that the desired deliverance has actually arrived, since, coming after the thanksgiving, it appears to imply that the condition of the speaker after the deliverance is just the same as it was before it. All the attempts so far made to get over this difficulty have about them an air of desperation.[5]

Simply, Cranfield argues that verse 25 is the key as the "wretched man" thanks God for his deliverance "through Jesus Christ" while, as one delivered in Christ, still struggling to overcome "the law of sin" in his "flesh."

The words considered over the course of church history with regards to indwelling sin are found principally in Romans 7:21–23, "So I find it to be a law that when I want to do right, evil lies close at hand. For I delight in the law of God, in my inner being, but I see in my members another law waging war against the law of my mind and making me captive to the law of sin that dwells in my members."

Paul uses the word "law" in a few different ways and part of the problem of interpretation involves understanding in what precise sense he is speaking of it here. According to John Owen, "A law is taken either properly for a *directive rule*, or improperly for an *operative effective principle*, which seems to have the force of a law."[6]

The law, considered as a directive, is a moral rule given in order to influence and command a person's will concerning what is either commanded or forbidden. Very often rewards and penalties are attached to the obedience to or transgression of a law. God offered such a law in the garden to Adam and, over the course of redemptive history, He gave many laws that both threatened and promised. Positive laws, moral laws, ceremonial laws, and civil laws all fall under the category of "directive rules."

The law, considered as an inward principle, will incline the will toward certain actions. The "law of the Spirit of life" sets those in Christ apart from the "law of sin and death" (Rom. 8:2). The word "law" here is being used in terms of an inward principle. Likewise, in Romans 7:21, 23 (but not v. 22), Paul seems to be using the word "law" to denote an inward principle that helps us understand the nature of indwelling sin. Owen speaks of indwelling sin as "a powerful and effectual indwelling principle, inclining and pressing unto actions agreeable and suitable unto its own nature. . . . Now, that which we observe from this name or term of a 'law' attributed unto sin is, That *there is an exceeding efficacy and power in the remainders of indwelling sin in believers, with a constant working towards evil.*"[7] Remaining in us is a certain "law." The dominion of sin is broken, so that the strength of original sin is truly weakened. In Christ, we are able now to mortify sin by the Spirit (Rom. 8:13); but this "law" still works with great power. And, truly, as Owen reminds us: "Where it is least felt, it is most powerful."[8] Perhaps paradoxically, those who feel most the strength of indwelling sin are those who least need to worry. As Owen says, "They that find not its power are under its dominion."[9]

Yet, in every true child of God, because the Spirit lives within us, we will necessarily live to God with a constant desire to please Him, despite the fact that indwelling sin remains in us. Owen says that believers in their so-called worst condition are still distinguished from unbelievers in their so-called best condition.[10] When an unbeliever "fights" against sin, he or she does so due to the remaining light of nature in conscience—which is truly a gift (of common grace) from God to this world. The desire of the godless to sin is not eradicated, but only restrained by various means. Their obedience to various good laws is not because of a holy disposition. They do not have a renewed will, which means their moral actions are only consistent with their natural will.

Believers, however, because they are alive to God in Christ by the Spirit, have a perpetual—not perfect—inclination to the good. In other words, they do not wake up one day without any inclination to what is good and the next day a reversal of attitude toward the virtuous. Yet, as Owen notes, indwelling sin is "effectually operative in rebelling and inclining to evil, when the will of doing good is in a particular manner active and inclining unto obedience."[11] For the believer, we have two principles within us, which war against each other. The good that we wish to do is from the Spirit dwelling in us as new creatures in Christ, which means it is, as noted above, perpetual. But we must also recognize that "the desires of the flesh are against the Spirit, and the desires of the Spirit are against the flesh, for these are opposed to each other, to keep you from doing the things you want to do" (Gal. 5:17; see also 1 Peter 2:11). This is the summary of the Christian life: not passive reluctance to our sin, but a holy war waged by one who knows that victory is assured because "he who is in you is greater than he who is in the world" (1 John 4:4).

DOMINION OF SIN

Because God is God and we are His creatures, we are necessarily under His moral law. This is true of every human being who has ever lived. We are under this law from the moment of our conception. We owe to God and our neighbor love, which is the fulfillment of the law (Rom. 13:8–10). Both being "in Adam" (Rom. 5) and also our failure to perfectly love God and our neighbor are the reasons for our condemnation and guilt before God.

But by nature we are also under another law: the dominion of sin. It is an internal "law," not an external command that directs us to how we ought to act. This inward principle or law impels us. The moral law given to Adam had this same type of force. Before sin, he was impelled toward God and His commandments. Now, because of original sin, all we have are the "sparks" of this moral law remaining in us. We desperately need God to write His law freshly upon our hearts by His grace (Heb. 10:16). But even when God renews us in the image of His Son (Rom. 8:29), we still have an indwelling principle that inclines us toward sin.

Various aspects of indwelling sin require explanation for us to understand its nature. Indwelling sin is ever with us in this life; it never leaves us until we depart to be with Christ. The soul is the home of indwelling sin. As Owen says,

> There it dwells, and is no wanderer. Wherever you are, whatever you are about, this law of sin is always in you; in the best that you do, and in the worst. Men little consider what a dangerous companion is always at home with them. When they are in company, when alone, by night or by day, all is one, sin is with them. There is a living coal continually in their houses; which, if it be not looked unto, will fire them, and it may be consume them.[12]

We should never forget there is an enemy that walks around with us, pretending very often to be our best friend while truly being our worst enemy.

Indwelling sin is always ready to pounce. It is not lazy, though it breeds laziness. As Paul says, "Evil lies close at hand" (Rom. 7:21) because sin dwells in him (Rom. 7:17). Sin does not simply dwell in us, but it is close at hand, aiming to disrupt our living to God. This "law" dwells in us as a principle that never entirely takes a holiday from our actions (Heb. 12:1). Owen speaks about the reality of indwelling sin in the life of a Christian: "Would you pray . . . would you meditate, would you be in any duty acting faith on God and love towards him, would you work righteousness, would you resist temptations,—this troublesome, perplexing indweller will still more or less put itself upon you and be present with you; so that you cannot perfectly and completely accomplish the thing that is good, as our apostle speaks" (Romans 7:18).[13]

This principle needs no helper to act, though sometimes the world or the devil join with it in its destructive cause. There is a certain "ease" with which it acts in us; it is always eating but never full.

ENMITY IN THE HEART

The Scriptures constantly bear witness to the problem of the heart (Gen. 6:5; Eccl. 9:3; Matt. 15:19). The will and the heart are so intricately bound up that they are essentially one. That is why the heart must be remedied for our actions to be fixed. The heart may also represent the mind, affections, conscience, and soul. "The soul who sins shall die" could equally be "the heart that sins shall die" (Ezek. 18:20).

The heart is where our enemy (sin) dwells, and the place from which rebellion arises. Sin raises its ugly head with the temptation sometimes leading to sin and sometimes resisted. Whether we give in or conquer, indwelling sin will always be present to return again and again because the heart is never, in this life, fully rid of its presence. As John Newton (1725–1807) says, "My heart is like a country but half subdued, where all things are in an unsettled state, and mutinies and insurrections are daily happening."[14] A Trojan horse remains in our heart, with enemies inside ready to pounce.

Remaining sin manifests ongoing enmity against God (Rom. 8:7). Even the smallest degree of enmity against God is still enmity. Whether a glass or a drop, poison is still poison. We mortify sin so that the force of it is subdued. And even in the very height of our progressive sanctification on earth, the nature of sin does not change. Sin hates the holiness of God, as they are the most distant from each other in all of the created universe.

This enmity works itself out in terms of an aversion to God. Why is prayer so difficult for the Christian? Because indwelling sin constantly fights against spiritual duties such as private or public communion with God. As powerfully as we may (sometimes) feel the Spirit at work in our obedience to God, we can never shake off the shackles of the remaining enemy within. In other words, there is never a time when we can perform a truly perfect, sinless act toward an infinitely holy God. He knows our affections are always, to a certain degree, divided. How often is our mind set upon an act of worship toward God and we quickly feel pulled toward things unrelated to the immediate task at hand? This is because of indwelling sin and the war it wages upon us at every opportunity.

As Christians, while we are not under the dominion of sin, we affirm that we are in a battle with sin. We are, as Paul says, to "make no provision for the flesh, to gratify its desires" (Rom. 13:14). These desires of the flesh are opposed to the Spirit, and they try to keep us from doing that which is holy and pleasing to God (Gal. 5:17). Being kind to our sin is being mean to ourselves.

At this point we should be careful to distinguish between how a heart may have a perpetual and habitual inclination toward sin versus a perpetual and habitual inclination of the law of sin that remains in a sanctified heart. The former is true of unbelievers whereas the latter is true of believers. Owen makes this basic point: "The heart is not habitually inclined unto evil by the remainders of indwelling sin; but this sin in the heart has a constant, habitual propensity unto evil in itself or its own nature."[15] So while we are not always only sinning, we do always, in this life, have the propensity to sin at any time.

EFFECTS UPON THE REGENERATE

Because of indwelling sin, we must be aware as Christians of its effects on us and how it assaults us. A few effects are worthy of consideration, particularly since knowing the way our sin attacks us will help us better understand the nature of the Christian life.

In every believer there are what Owen calls "unexpected surprisals," which arise in the soul in the form of "foolish, sinful figments and imaginations."[16] We need not look for these types of sinful thoughts or even place ourselves in a particular context for them to take place. Instead, thoughts and affections that are contrary to God's law "surprise" the soul. Lusts of various kinds can spring up "involuntarily" in the heart; though, they are, strictly speaking, voluntary, since sin resides in the will.

Sin can attack at any moment. We can, like a king in a palace, fortify ourselves with many guards and protections, but we need to remember that no king is truly safe when his enemies are within the gates, so to speak. Sin surprises us in various ways. For example, we may be aiming to repent for a particular sin and then be carried away by that sin with a fresh delight in it. We can at times move from repentance to sin with more ease than from sin to repentance. Indwelling sin has perpetual propensity in and of itself to raise terror to the soul. And this prevents us from ever being in a position where we can relax and take our hand off of our sword in the Christian life. This is why the life of denial is a daily taking up of the cross, not a weekly or yearly one (Luke 9:23).

Indwelling sin loves temptation and the opportunity it provides to get to work. When we are tempted, we fight not simply the outward temptation but the inward recesses of our heart that see the temptation with eyes of delight. The Lord was tempted, argues Owen, more "intensively and extensively, in number, quality, and fierceness, from Satan and the world," than any other person. Yet in all of these temptations "he had to deal only with that which came from without."[17] We deal with that which arises from within the heart and find, all too often, a constant willingness to give in to various temptations. We get no holidays in the Christian life, no days off. We cannot even enjoy a minute when sin agrees to leave us alone. That does not mean that we are always sinning, but it does mean sin is always lurking in the shadows ready to attack.

Indwelling sin proposes to the mind and affections that which is evil. We are not responsible or guilty for outward temptations unless we consent to them. But, because of indwelling sin, sinful lusts and proposals from within are our moral responsibility, and so must be mortified (Rom. 8:13). We cannot be blamed for an outward temptation, which is why our Lord was free from sin despite facing many and varied temptations Himself. But the act of the soul that yearns after that which is evil is sin. For example, an inward temptation toward idolatry, sexual immorality, or homosexuality, even if not acted upon outwardly, is a sin, for it involves a desire after things not agreeable to God's law. A sin can be exacerbated if the lust is unnatural. In addition, a man who has lustful desires toward a woman, and meditates on committing them, even though there is no formal outward act, is also guilty—he is even more guilty if he is married and the other woman (not his wife) is also married. And, moving away from sexual temptations of various sorts, someone may solicit us to cheat, steal, or lie, which would not be a sin if we resisted that overture; but our desire to cheat, steal, or lie, even if not acted upon, renders us guilty of sin. Thus the need for the grace of God to wash us of our sin and give us power to have Christ shape our minds to things agreeable to His will. God gives specific commands. For example, we are not merely to love our neighbor in some undefined manner. God explains how this love manifests itself; in the sixth commandment, as in other commandments also, we are both to refrain from harming and killing our neighbor while also seeking to promote the health and welfare of our neighbor. Finding the time, energy, and resources to help someone is difficult because indwelling sin weakens our desire to help as we should, and very often keeps us from doing what we should. As Paul says, "For I do not do the good I want, but the evil I do not want is what I keep on doing. Now if I do what I do not want, it is no longer I who do it, but sin that dwells within me" (Rom. 7:19–20). Even if one is able to prove in this particular instance that Paul is not speaking as a Christian, is it not true that the commanded good we know to do is very often not accomplished?

APPLICATION

The power of indwelling sin is great. In Christ, we will certainly win the victory in the end over this obstinate and powerful enemy, but we must wage continual war with that great foe that remains within us until we depart to be with the Lord. A holy Christian is always sensitive to the power of sin. We know that sin has defeated us many times in our lives. We might be aware of a sin rising up in the soul, mind, and heart, but soon after mortify it. Other times, we act on the temptation and the lusts arising in our hearts. Regarding these failures, whether internal only or external also, only true believers feel sorrow and hatred from what remains in them coupled with the desire to turn to God and away from sin.

Ignorance of the nature of indwelling sin leads to a failure to prepare for the battle against it that rages in our souls and tests the loyalty of soldiers of Christ. A violent enemy resides as an unwanted guest within every Christian. This foe may be crushed in its first rising by the Spirit, but it will return again and again. Do not be unaware of the "resurrection" power of sin. It may seem to die, but it comes back to life, at times with a vengeance and more vicious and cleverer than experienced at first. We are dealing not only with a powerful enemy but a cunning one within us.

The gospel opens our eyes to Christ and God's truth, but sin keeps us from seeing clearly and acting sinlessly. John Duncan reminds us that, even in our state of grace, we can never boast of a sinless action: "I have never done a sinless action during the seventy years [of my life]. I don't say but by God's grace there may have been some holy action done, but never a sinless action during the seventy years. What an awful thing is human life! And what a solemn consideration it should be to us, that we have never done a sinless action all our life, that we have never done one act that did not need to be pardoned."[18] We must recognize that, in this life, the most holy act possible is tainted by sin. That does not mean God does not accept it and reward it due to His mercy and grace in Christ. But it does mean we should be realistic about what we can offer in this life in our service to and for the glory of the triune God.

6

SIN'S SORROW: HARD TO SAY I'M SORRY

SPEAK EVIL OF EVIL

Can we speak too terribly of sin? The American Reformed theologian William G. T. Shedd (1820–94) correctly remarked, "Human character is worthless in proportion as abhorrence of sin is lacking in it."[1] To the degree that people hate sin they reflect the image of God in them and thus they flee idolatry (1 Cor. 10:14).

When we talk of it, we include all the evils it encompasses. Thomas Goodwin declared, "If all evils were to have an excrement, a scum, a superfluity, sin is it, and being the abstracted quintessence of all evil—an evil which, in nature and essence of it, virtually, and eminently contains all evils of what kind soever that are in the world."[2] This evil is in us. This is a terrifying thought, so much so that we try with all of our might to extinguish the reality of our natural inward perversities. We do not even know what we really are by nature or what we are capable of doing. Out of His grace, God preserves us from seeing ourselves in a manner that might cause an instant heart attack. But God also, according to His saving grace, allows His children to see themselves as sinners truly, albeit partially, that they may flee to Christ for cleansing and salvation.

When we speak of mourning over our own sins, certain non-negotiable truths should always be uppermost in our minds. Lamenting sin is only of value when it is evangelical; that is, it is a fruit of the grace of repentance, which comes as a gift from God. Superficial mourning or sorrow over sin leads only to death (2 Cor. 7:10). But we must remember that if we differ from someone else as true "mourners," we cannot claim to be better in and of ourselves. Who makes us to differ from the world insofar as we mourn over our sins whereas the pagans do not? God alone, through Christ, by the Spirit.

ALL INFECTED EQUALLY

Adam's sin affected all of his natural descendants. Likewise, he conveyed sin to all his posterity not in part but the whole. Charnock observes that man, without exception or distinction, "is so wretched by nature, that nothing but what is vile and pernicious can drop from him."[3] This corruption springing from Adam to us all is "equal to all, natural to all; it is not more poisonous or more fierce in one man than in another. The root of all men is the same; all the branches therefore do equally possess the villainous nature of the root. No child of Adam can by natural descent be better than Adam."[4] This common Reformed position qualifies itself regarding how this mutual and monstrous root expresses itself. Thus the only thing keeping one man from being as bad as he could be by nature is God's restraining grace, which is not equal to all. Some are restrained by various means more than others.

Goodwin likewise says that "all concupiscence is in every man's nature. Sin, [Paul] says here, that is, Original Sin, wrought all concupiscence [strong, inordinate lust], and of that we are partakers all alike."[5] We all possess and share the same sin nature. We are all slaves to sin, not just particular sins. Particular sins, such as theft or lying, are the result of the sin nature present in each of us. These acts differ from person to person, but the sin nature we have inherited from our father,

Adam, is not less or more for each person. Goodwin adds Adam's sin has "the same and like impression upon all men's hearts." As a result, left to ourselves, we are prone to all sins: "For the influence of [sin] is not as the influence of a voluntary, but a natural agent, which always works [to the ultimate power], and therefore conveys the same image to all that it does to any, because it works to the utmost of its power."[6] The grace of God is given freely, which means even in the work of sanctification we are not all alike as holy, though we share the designation "holy." But sin affects all necessarily, and therefore one cannot claim to be, by nature, better than another person. If there is any outward morality whereby one pagan surpasses another, it is purely due to the common work of God's grace. God is free to restrain as He pleases for His inscrutable purposes.

Regarding actual sins, each person differs from the next; but original sin remains equal in all. Manton declares, "All the sins that ever have been or shall be committed in the world, they are virtually in our natures, they are but Original Sin acted and drawn out this way and that way . . . and if we were but left to ourselves, and had the same temptations and occasions, we should be as bad as others; such as we would not imagine that ever we should commit is in our heart."[7] Whatever actual sin we can conceive, the power to do so lies in each heart apart from the grace of God. There is no sin we could not theoretically commit.

As we think of history's most evil people, we should remember that we share the same foundational malignancy as they. God alone can cure us, and that cure He administers voluntarily to whom He chooses. Adam was the one who infected all of us except Christ, who alone escapes its ravages. As Manton observes, "The root of all the mischief which has been in the world is within us."[8] Charnock also testifies, "The best men have the worst sins in their nature, though, by grace, they have them not in their practice."[9] Did you refrain from murdering someone today? Such restraint came from God whose grace alone kept you from prison and your upcoming murder trial.

INDIVIDUAL MOURNING

Through the power of the gospel, the dominion of sin is broken in the Christian (Rom. 6:14). But the presence of sin remains, and we refer to it as "indwelling sin" in the believer. More will be said on this, but for now, we must recognize that while we are gloriously forgiven in Christ, we will always in this life need to lament our remaining indwelling sin.

The Bible abounds with examples of mourning over one's sins. David's lamentations over his sin are well described in Psalm 51 (esp. vv. 1–4) and very well known in the church. But he is far from alone. The ways in which God's people have confessed their unworthiness before God are many and varied. Sometimes it is not a straightforward confession of sin, but with the basic idea present. Jacob, for example, confessed: "I am not worthy of the least of all the deeds of steadfast love and all the faithfulness that you have shown to your servant" (Gen. 32:10). The ones sensitive to their sin are also sensitive to all the good that God shows them. Such people know they do not deserve even the least of God's kind acts toward them. Likewise, in the presence of God, His saints possess an awareness of God's matchless holiness and how it exposes their great uncleanness. For example, Isaiah saw the glory of Christ (see John 12:41), and he was "undone": "Woe is me! For I am lost; for I am a man of unclean lips, and I dwell in the midst of a people of unclean lips; for my eyes have seen the King, the LORD of hosts!" (Isa. 6:5). Consider Peter as well, who, when confronted with Christ's Messianic glory in the catching of a great number of fish, fell at Christ's knees, saying, "Depart from me, for I am a sinful man, O Lord" (Luke 5:8).

We, like David, should be able to say often and fervently: "I acknowledged my sin to you, and I did not cover my iniquity" (Ps. 32:5).

Or, "I confess my iniquity; I am sorry for my sin" (Ps. 38:18). "If we say we have no sin," John warns us, "we deceive ourselves, and the truth is not in us" (1 John 1:8). When the truth is in us, the truth about who we are must be confessed. And since we still sin, we will naturally hate that we do so. The great Scottish preacher, Robert Murray M'Cheyne (1813–43), offers what may appear to us today in the twenty-first century to be an excessive harshness regarding himself, but I think we need to seek for ourselves his holy hatred of personal sin:

> I daily wish that sin had been rooted out of my heart. I say, "Why did God leave the roots of lasciviousness, pride, anger, &c., in my bosom? He hates sin, and I hate it." . . . If I were more deeply convinced of my utter helplessness, I think I would not be so alarmed when I hear of the falls of other men. . . . I should study those sins in which I am most helpless, in which passion becomes like a whirlwind and I like a straw. No figure of speech can represent my utter want of power to resist the torrent of sin.[10]

Loving God necessarily means hating our sin. We love what God loves, and we hate what God hates. The more we love God, the more we will hate our sin. And since we still have remaining sin, we will hate its presence with a holy detestation that should lead us back to love for God in Christ.

GODLY SORROW

"No man is born with godly sorrow in his heart, as he is born with a tongue in his mouth," observes Thomas Brooks.[11] Such sorrow must be altogether supernatural insofar as it emerges as a "plant of God's own planting; it is a seed of his own sowing . . . it is a heavenly offspring; it is from God, and God alone. The Spirit of mourning is from above; it is from a supernatural power and principle."[12] The Westminster Shorter Catechism therefore speaks of repentance as a divinely gifted "saving grace" (A. 87). The act of repentance belongs to the sinner, but its power comes from God. We must mourn over sin, but we can only do so with a spirit of repentance, which, declares Watson, "gives the soul a vomit."[13]

Our sorrow over our sins is a sorrow for sin as it truly is, sin. Speaking of the time before Augustine's conversion he tells of his attitude in the famous pear-stealing incident; he sensed the foul evil within, yet still loved it (Book 2, section 4). He says, "I loved my own perdition and my own faults, not the things for which I committed wrong, but the wrong itself." He loved sin as sin, not just the specific act whereby his sin terminated (e.g., stealing). The opposite becomes the case for the godly: we lament our sin as sin.

Additionally, sin brings many disadvantages, losses, punishments, etc., but we cannot simply mourn over these things. Even the world mourns over losses that happen as a result of sin. Godly sorrow takes man the offender beyond to God the offended (Ps. 51:4). It transcends sorrow for the consequences for sin by recognizing, from the heart, that one's offense is always against God. David's "heart struck him" when he was convicted that the census he took was sinful. He lamented, "I have sinned greatly in what I have done. But now, O LORD, please take away the iniquity of your servant, for I have done very foolishly" (2 Sam. 24:10).

Godly sorrow not only comes from the heart, but one bathed in humility. Charnock warns us, "Pride is a preparation for judgment; the higher the tower aspires, the fitter tinder it is for lightning; the bigger anything swells, the nearer it is to bursting; the prouder any man is, the plainer butt he is for an arrow of God's wrath."[14] In Isaiah 57:15, we encounter the exalted and eternal Lord, dwelling "in the high and holy place" who dwells with the "contrite and lowly [in] spirit" who see themselves for what they are (with their sin) and God for who He is (in His holiness). God will "revive" such broken hearts; He demands such as His dwelling place.

Our sorrow for our own sin puts us in the right position to properly feel sorrow for the sins of others. We cannot, in humility, lament the sins of another person if we have not also lamented what remains in us. We ought to be careful not to be like the hypocrite, who fails to take the log out of his own eye while trying to take the speck out of the eye of a brother (Matt. 7:4–5). My sin, like a telephone pole sticking out of my eye-socket, remains a bigger problem than the sawdust particle in my brother's eye. Why? My sin is my biggest problem, because it is my sin. I must hate it and deal with it if I would ever properly address the sin of others in true grace.

Godly sorrow is also a comforting sorrow. True sorrow for sin leads to repentance, which leads us back to Christ. There is no godly sorrow without a return to Him who pities and sympathizes with us in our weaknesses (Heb. 4:15). Our Lord promised us, "Blessed are those who mourn, for they shall be comforted" (Matt. 5:4). The goal of mourning is comfort. In fact, we may even join godly sorrow with godly joy. They are, due to the mystery of grace in Christ, friends, not enemies. Brooks declares, "The higher the springs of godly sorrow rise, the higher the tides of holy joy rise. His graces will flourish most, who evangelically mourns most."[15]

The sorrow we have over our sins must be over sins great and small. We cannot excuse certain sins because they are not significant to us. No sin before God is a little thing. Jesus died for all of our sins, which means all of our sins are weighty before Almighty God. Brooks cautions,

An unsound heart may mourn for great sins, that make great wounds in his conscience and credit, and that leave a great blot upon his name . . . or expose him to public scorn and shame . . . but for sins of omission, for wandering thoughts, idle words,

79

deadness, coldness, slightness in religious duties and services, unbelief, secret pride, self-confidence, and a thousand more, such gnats as these he can swallow without any remorse.[16]

We must confess our particular sins as well as our general sinfulness before God. Deceit lies hidden in the generals, and our deceitful hearts cause us to omit dealing with our very specific faults. But we should also remember that as we look at our specific sins, they arise not in a vacuum but out of our indwelling sinfulness.

APPLICATION

Godly sorrow over our sin is not a popular topic of teaching in pulpits today. Indeed, many have rightly lamented this failure throughout church history. The North American evangelical church today suffers by not stressing godly sorrow in our Christian experience and, as a result, also missing a certain type of godly joy that accompanies such sorrow. For such sorrow brings us to God, through Christ, by the Spirit. Pray earnestly for this sorrow over your sin and for preaching that cultivates such a spiritual disposition.

As Christians we should also remember that only the grace of God makes us differ from the vilest sinner in the world. It should humble us to our core to know that, given the right time and circumstances, we could have been a Hitler or a Stalin. This does not deny human responsibility for our actions; but all humanity shares the natural infection and terminal disease of sin, which can only be cured by the triune God. By God's grace we can thank Him and rejoice that we are not what we used to be or what we could be. Still, we must remember the sin that remains and mourn over what could destroy our lives completely apart from the mercy of God in Christ.

Finally, it is one thing to read the Psalms of David, but quite another thing to experience them. God permits us to sin—not with any approval, of course—and our reaction is crucial. Consider David in Psalm 38. He lacks health in his bones, because of his sin (v. 3); his foolishness has humbled him (v. 6), moving him to lament, "I am utterly bowed down and prostrate; all the day I go about mourning" (v. 6). He later adds, regarding his sin, "I confess my iniquity; I am sorry for my sin" (v. 18). But by the end, God knows that David truly desires him:

> Do not forsake me, O LORD!
> O my God, be not far from me!
> Make haste to help me,
> O Lord, my salvation! (vv. 21–22)

Is God the God of our salvation? By the grace of the Father, for the sake of the Son, and by the power of the Holy Spirit, He is in not only our God in our righteousness but also in our confessed sinfulness. We can all confess with John Newton, "I remember two things: that I am a great sinner and that Christ is a great Savior."[17]

But remember, as John Owen perceptively notes, "The great sin of believers is, that they make not use of Christ's bounty as they ought to do; that we do not every day take of him mercy in abundance."[18] This is one sin we cannot afford to continue to commit; He is too great a Savior for us not to rush to Him daily.

7

SIN'S ALTERNATIVE: HURTS SO GOOD

CHOICES

We all face many choices in life, some practical and some purely hypothetical. Regarding the latter, we can often give the right theological answer, but betray our "theology" with practical decisions that contradict God's truth. Indeed, a Christian theist may live like a practical atheist by disregarding God and failing to worship Him in Spirit and in truth. To the degree that our lives are reflective of the truth, we are in the safest place. At times, our decisions and beliefs may appear stupid and senseless to the world, but faith in God and His Word directs us on a course that ultimately leads to glory and blessing, joy and comfort.

In one of the most penetrating books written in English on sin during the Puritan era, Jeremiah Burroughs (1600–1646) discusses an issue that may be framed in the following question: faced between choosing the smallest sin versus the greatest affliction, which should the Christian choose? He starts out his magnificent treatise arguing "that any affliction is to be chosen rather than any sin; that there is more evil in any sin, the least sin, than in the greatest affliction."[1] With Burroughs, because of our belief in the God in the Scriptures, we should hold that it is better to be "under the greatest affliction [than] be under the guilt of power of sin."[2] Why? Because, as we shall see, William Gurnall (1616–79) was right to say, "God's wounds cure,—sin's kisses kill."[3]

TEMPORARY VERSUS ETERNAL

Hell would not exist if there were no sin, but even the smallest sin means that, apart from the satisfaction of Christ, it awaits anyone who has committed even one of even the smallest sins. Hell is a place of misery and affliction; yet, says Burroughs, there is "more evil in the least sin than in all the miseries that . . . a creature is capable of, either here or in Hell."[4]

Consider, as well, hell is the place of eternal torment, but the afflictions of believers on earth are temporary. The apostle Paul clearly stated, "For this light momentary affliction is preparing for us an eternal weight of glory beyond all comparison" (2 Cor. 4:17). This mirrors what he said in Romans 8:18: "For I consider that the sufferings of this present time are not worth comparing with the glory that is to be revealed to us." Our afflictions, however painful they may be, are not even worth comparing to what awaits us in glory.

The consequences for sin are, however, eternal. As believers, our afflictions last only a short lifetime, but a moment compared to eternal glory we will receive. For anyone outside Christ, the wages of sin is death (Rom. 6:23), which brings the enemy of God into separation from Him forever. False professors of the faith, whose works were purely outward and not from the heart by faith, will enter eternal punishment (Matt. 25:46). Rightly choosing affliction over sin takes the long look to the wages of each. Sin leads to death and torment, but affliction leads to life and glory.

Consider the promises offered to each in the motivation to prefer affliction over sin. In Isaiah, God promises exiled Israel in their affliction:

"When you pass through the waters, I will be with you;
    and through the rivers, they shall not overwhelm you;
when you walk through fire you shall not be burned,
    and the flame shall not consume you." (Isa. 43:2)

We can be assured that in our afflictions we are being tried by a faithful God. Afflictions are likewise a sign of His faithfulness, which sometimes shows His fatherly discipline. As the psalmist says, "I know, O LORD, that your rules are righteous, and that in faithfulness you have afflicted me" (119:75). Notice, for example, that Paul's great promise in Romans 8:28, that all things work together for good for those who love God, emerges out of a context of suffering (Rom. 8:18–27). There exist no such promises for sin, but only threats and warnings: "For in the day that you eat of it you shall surely die" (Gen. 2:17).

God makes our afflictions the signs of our sonship. As adopted children, our chastisements and afflictions show God's goodness and mercy toward us. If He left us alone, we would surely ignore Him and perhaps only turn to Him occasionally. God disciplines His children, those whom He loves (Heb. 12:6). When God treats us as children rather than illegitimate offspring, we can be sure of many things, such as His love and forgiveness. But we can also know that He will not overindulge those who drift away from Him. He disciplines us as true children (Heb. 12:7–8). Returning to the promises for the afflicted, we see that God's fatherly discipline "yields the peaceful fruit of righteousness to those who have been trained by it" (Heb. 12:11). Rather than simply removing the problems and plagues of this world, God uses them to make us like His Son.

We are blessed therefore in affliction, but sin offers no such promise of blessing. Consider the psalmist: "Blessed is the man whom you discipline, O LORD, and whom you teach out of your law" (Ps. 94:12). Affliction teaches us God's ways (Ps. 119:71). Sin cannot in itself bring forth good, but affliction can when received by faith. The sin Joseph's brothers committed against him was evil, but his patient suffering at the hand of God brought about good not only in his life but also the lives of others; all of this in spite of and beyond the wicked treatment. As we see preeminently in the case of our Lord, the fruit of the Spirit in affliction makes it good. When God does not afflict, then it may be a sign of His judgment rather than His love (see Hos. 4:14).

INCAPABLE OF GOOD

When we live by faith, we can accept our afflictions, but the person living by faith can never accept sins. Thus, we must always choose afflictions over sin. Consider Moses, who, by faith, "when he was grown up, refused to be called the son of Pharaoh's daughter, choosing rather to be mistreated with the people of God than to enjoy the fleeting pleasures of sin" (Heb. 11:24–25). At the end, Moses claimed that his afflictions were good for him, but not his sin. Of course, we may realize, sometimes painfully, that our course of action will lead to affliction if we are righteous; and perhaps we deceive ourselves by thinking a little sin, as well as the covering of it, will prevent afflictions. This may be the case, humanly speaking. But faith knows that afflictions, including those that come as a result of sin, are not evil. On the contrary, sin is evil and believers can rejoice in suffering, knowing that they escape greater suffering that comes because of sin. Sin often provides an immediate way out of a problem only for us to encounter many more problems than anticipated. This is because sin cannot beget goodness, but only misery.

Regarding the vain quest of men to get something good out of sin, Burroughs warns: "All those good ends that any men have in the commission of sin, yet do not make their sin the better: that cannot make sin good, because they have good ends."[5] Perhaps a person may think that a small sin can help with a larger temptation. Someone might say, "One quick look at this website and the lustful desire will go away." But this is playing with fire! In the process, the conscience loses sensitivity to the guilt and danger of these alleged "small sins" and they are even excused as something good.

Imagine a hypothetical scenario whereby a small sin may do a greater good. Burroughs actually raises this issue: "If a man might be a means to save the whole world if he would commit one sin, if he could save the whole world from eternal torments by the commission of one sin, you should suffer the whole world to perish rather than commit one sin, there is so much evil in sin."[6] Should we commit a small sin to save the whole world or, closer to home, a loved one? The answer, to the protest of what seems right in our own eyes, must be an emphatic, "No!" Otherwise, sin would then have the glory. Jesus was tempted by the devil in this way. Satan offered Jesus all the authority and glory that had been delivered to him (Luke 4:6). Jesus simply had to worship Satan, and it would all be Christ's (Luke 4:7). If Jesus had bowed, Satan would get the honor for his "gift" to the Son, whereas the Father's promises to the Son depended on His faithfulness to the Father, not Satan. Jesus chose wisely, taking the path of affliction rather than sin. His whole life could be summed up as a faithful choice for the greatest affliction over the smallest sin. Our salvation depended on this choice. He knew that sin and the devil were incapable of delivering on their false promises.

MOST CONTRARY TO GOD

Another reason we should choose affliction and suffering over sin is that sin is the most opposite to God. As we think of God in His infinite goodness—and what a truly meager understanding we have—we may rightly conclude that only sin is truly contrary and opposite to God. As Burroughs argued, "God hath no object that he can look upon contrary to himself in all the world, but only sin."[7] Jesus, who knew no sin, was afflicted and chose affliction rather than sin. He could not sin, because

He is a divine person, not two persons. The smallest taint of sin in God would render Him the most reprehensible being in the universe, worse than the devil. The evil in the devil is limited by his finite being. God, however, is infinite. So, sin in God would mean He would be infinitely sinful with an infinite power and terrifying beyond our wildest, darkest, and most disgusting conception of despair. Of course, sin in our infinitely and unchangeably holy and just God is impossible and we should shudder to even contemplate His divine majesty in any way tainted with sin.

Sin is not only contrary to God in the fact that it is most evil and He is most good, but also as it continually works against Him. Sin is a restless evil. It is not lazy as we may be, since even in our laziness sin is working ever so hard. Sin means we walk contrary to God, which is a perilous thing indeed: "Then if you walk contrary to me and will not listen to me, I will continue striking you, sevenfold for your sins" (Lev. 26:21). When God's people walked contrary to God, He threatened to walk contrary to them, and threatened His people because of their sin (Lev. 26:24–30). We should choose anything except to walk contrary to God, even if that means affliction.

There can be no friendship between God and sin because the hierarchy of authority in this universe can never be undone. God is the majestic sovereign, but sin does not care for this order of authority. When we willfully oppose God and His law, we make a claim upon His authority with an unholy usurpation of the grossest sort. It does not matter what sin is committed. True, there are degrees of sin, "but," as Burroughs says, "every sin is invenomed with the same evil: That which is the venom of any one sin, is the venom of all; all comes from the same root."[8] The same poison gives rise to every sin, though there may be more poison in some sins. But we should remember that in our understanding of sin, we are never in the best position to evaluate how truly horrible it is. Our sympathy to sin, because of indwelling sin, never allows us to come close to 20/20 vision in terms of seeing sin clearly. Burroughs adds that "God does not account sin only according to man's intentions in sinning; what man intends, but what the nature of the sin tends unto, not what I do aim at in my sinning, but what my sin does aim at."[9] Choosing the greatest suffering over the smallest sin should therefore be understood in light of this principle: a "small sin" is still a grievous evil. God fully comprehends the horror of the "small sin." Our duty as Christians is to aspire, so far as it is possible and by the power of the Spirit, to the same view of sin as our Lord and Maker.

APPLICATION

By God's grace, we must get this truth into our heads and hearts: Choosing suffering over sin is better because all sin involves suffering anyway. Richard Sibbes (1577–1635) was right to say, "It is better to go bruised to heaven than sound to hell."[10]

Part of the folly of sin concerns the assumption that it can be experienced without consequences. Living by faith, in obedience to God, means we can trust Him to be faithful to us in our afflictions. Choosing sin instead essentially admits, "I am choosing all of the serious consequences that come with my sin." The earthly consequences are painful and often impossible to eradicate.

Choosing suffering over sin is choosing to live like our Savior. When we walk as He did, in the power of the Holy Spirit, we trust our Father and count on His help. In our call to suffer with Jesus as our example, like Him we can entrust all things and ourselves to our Father, "who judges justly" (1 Peter 2:21–23). Indeed, we can choose what is right because it is right. Yet as Christians we are promised so much more for our obedience than we can ever possibly deserve or even imagine. The simple thought that we are following in the footsteps of the Savior, albeit in a small way, should be enough for us.

This is not to understate the difficulty of the choices that come before God's people. A single pregnant woman contemplating an abortion is faced with this question: choose sin (murder) or affliction (public shame and economic hardship)? A father struggling to feed his family is tempted to steal. Does he choose a "small sin" hopefully without detection, or the hunger of his children? Does a child speak truthfully about recklessly breaking the window, with discipline to follow, or lie to escape punishment? These are the types of decisions many are faced with each day. Only by looking to God in Christ can we ever say, "I will choose (possible) affliction over the smallest sin."

When our eyes leave the Lord, we drift to living according to our own rules and dictates, which chooses the path of least resistance (sinning). Such an unwise choice initiates a confrontation against the God who graciously loves and saves us. He will love us still and, in the midst of such, pursue us and bring us back from our straying. One can never win against God. Yet, at the same time, in Christ, we can never lose when we seek His ways. As we think about God and Christ, the choice is always easy: do not choose sin, even if it means the greatest affliction.

SIN'S SECRECY: I PUT A SPELL ON YOU

PAUL'S PROBLEM

Richard Sibbes wrote, "For sin, like the devil, is afraid to appear in its own likeness, and men seek out fair glosses for foul intentions."[1] Sin does not like to be found out.

The natural man usually does not wish to be found guilty of public sins. True, some are so degenerate that they boast in their public sins, but many non-Christians love to be thought of as good, decent people. The difference between the desires of the non-Christian versus the Christian may be discerned by the desire for inward righteousness. Charnock notes, "Open impieties are refrained because of the eye of man, but secret sins are not checked because of the eye of God."[2] That is, God's omniscient eye is not enough to dissuade the wicked from committing sin because they are practical atheists, living as though God does not exist.

Paul after his conversion was different than he was before. Before his conversion, "as to righteousness under the law," he was blameless (Phil. 3:6). Internally, however, he was in a bad predicament: "But sin, seizing an opportunity through the commandment, produced in me all kinds of covetousness" (Rom. 7:8). His outward conduct was moral, but his heart was a boiling cauldron of covetousness that he could not control. These were his secret sins, which he and God knew about. Secret sins may not be a problem for us, except for the "inconvenient" fact that God knows our hearts better than we know them.

GOD SEES

When it comes to the matter of sin, one of the most fundamental truths a Christian must grasp concerns God's complete knowledge of all things. The infinite God has no limit to what He knows; He cannot learn, for He knows all things in and of Himself. He knows all things past, present, and future (Ps. 94:9–10; Isa. 46:8–11). He thus has a perfect knowledge of our sins, whether they be past, present, or future. From His perspective, no sin is secret.

The Christian knows that God is not ignorant of anything. We even ask God to search us, to know our hearts and thoughts, to show us any grievous ways in us (Ps. 139:23–24). Sometimes God's people can live and act as though God did not exist, and thus think their sins are hidden. Consider the leaders of Judah in Isaiah's time: "Ah, you who hide deep from the LORD your counsel, whose deeds are in the dark, and who say, 'Who sees us? Who knows us?'" (Isa. 29:15). We are not to imagine, therefore, that as professing Christians, we can act and live as though God is blind to our sins. Time and time again, we need to be reminded that all of our ways are before the Lord (Ps. 119:168); that "no creature is hidden from his sight, but all are naked and exposed to the eyes of him to whom we must give account" (Heb. 4:13).

Since God is everywhere present, knowing all things, we can never escape His all-seeing eye. We may, like Jonah, try to run from the Lord's presence (Jonah 1:3); or, like Adam and Eve, try to hide from God (Gen. 3:8). As practical atheists, we know God exists, but our actions betray such when we sin against His name and law and imagine He does not see us. In fact, when we sin, we don't want Him around.

SECRET SINS

What precisely are secret sins? In his work *The Anatomy of Secret Sins*, the Puritan Obadiah Sedgwick (1600–1658) offered a penetrating analysis of this particular manner of sinning. A secret sin may be one in which a person acts without a formal awareness of sinning, such as when Paul, in his zeal, persecuted the church. Also, a secret sin may refer to the manner of sinning. Some sins are "colored and disguised" as virtues.[3] Flattery may appear virtuous, but it is a lie designed for pernicious ends (e.g., control). Then there are sins "kept off from the stage of the world" and committed outside the public eye of the world.[4] A man may be an elder in a church but denigrate and abuse his wife and children in the privacy of his home without others knowing. Like John Bunyan's Talkative in *The Pilgrim's Progress*, he is a "saint abroad, and a devil at home."[5]

Finally, a secret sin may be one kept not only from the eyes of the public but also from any mortal's eyes. For example, at the secrecy of his computer, with the screen turned from others, a man may indulge in pornography without anyone in his home knowing. So, according to Sedgwick, "The carnal eye of him who commits the sins sees them not. He does indeed see them with the eye of conscience but not with an eye of natural sense: even those persons with whom he does converse, and who highly commend the frame of his ways, cannot yet see the secret discourse and acts of sin in his mind and heart."[6]

There are rumblings, like a violent volcano, that occur only in the heart of a person but do not manifest themselves in words or actions. Many have observed a beautiful mountain, not knowing that a pool of magma may be boiling and ready to emerge and destroy anything in its way. Our secret sins are not dangerous because man sees them, but because God sees them and knows their hidden foundation. Thomas Watson wrote, "Let me warn you this day not to sin in secret; know, that you can never sin so privately, but that there are always two witnesses by: God and conscience."[7]

INWARD DECEPTION

Secret sins are also dangerous because they deceive us. Indeed, all sin deceives to some extent, but secret sins are particularly dangerous when it comes to self-deception. We tend to judge our outward acts of sin more strictly than our inward sins, even excusing the latter because they did not become actual outward sins. Because we did not tell a certain person we find her reprehensible but only thought it instead (with hatred in our hearts), we imagine we have committed some act of righteousness by our restraint. So instead of being humbled for our thoughts, we actually applaud ourselves.

We also deceive ourselves with our sins by failing to understand what restrains us. We can hope that God's law and the Spirit of Christ dwelling in us will restrain us against actual sins, but very often we are held back by lesser means such as fear of shame and punishment. When it comes to secret sins, this reality will make us more apt to commit them, because there is no fear of shame and punishment when we think no one is watching (except God of course). We would never think of doing such things in front of others.

Sin is inward, but secret sins are "closest." They arise from original sin. As Sedgwick observes, "They are indeed Original Sin immediately acting itself, which sin is a full sin, a seeding sin, a sinning sin, and never weary."[8] From these carnal, fleshly heart-loves our actual sins flower. But if we are not going to commit actual sins, we may simply wish to enjoy the illicit loves of our hearts because, after all, no one is there to rebuke us and rain on our parade of sinful thoughts. The problem with this manner of living is rather startling, however. When a sin is acted upon it can, if not mortified, be repeated because we lose our sensitivity to the guilt and danger of sin. Our hearts become callous and our consciences are seared. A repeated sin, notes Sedgwick, turns into a "cable doubled in strength by the manifold twistings."[9] But secret sins are far more frequently replicated in our thoughts than actual sins. This leads to a strengthening of the various lustings in our hearts that are not easily undone except by true mortification of sin by the Spirit.

God looks upon us not as man does (1 Sam. 16:7). He searches the heart and requires real consequences for cherishing sin in our hearts. "If I had cherished iniquity in my heart," David reflects, "the Lord would not have listened" (Ps. 66:18). We can deceive others with what goes on in our hearts but is not acted upon outwardly, but we can never deceive God. For Christians, we not only should know this because of God's omniscience and omnipresence, but also because He actually dwells in us. In one sense, this is the problem for us: we cannot escape God's eye. But in another sense, this is the solution: the God who sees immediately can cleanse and restore us. Those who live in the Spirit will desire such inward cleansing. "Create in me a clean heart, O God, and renew a right spirit within me," is the cry of all true believers (Ps. 51:10; also see Matt. 5:8; Acts 15:9). In David's case, he was cleansed before the writing of Psalm 51, but he still desired it further. According to Sedgwick, David, as a whole man, "was cleansed," but he "was not cleansed wholly: some grace he had, but more he did want."[10] Those who have tasted the grace of God desire more. They are never satisfied that they have enough grace, but want more and more, because they increasingly hate the sin that remains in their being.

TRUE HATRED AND SADNESS

When we are made holy, it occurs inwardly before outwardly. Outward holiness without an internal change is hypocrisy, the stench of Pharisaical living that Jesus detests (Matt. 23:1–31). Unlike such formalists, we hate sin not simply because it is public or even private. Rather we hate sin as sin, both public and private, because it occurs against God and His glory. Hypocritical people, even professing Christians, typically worry about the consequences and shame of sin, and very often feel guilty with a natural guilt. But even such worries of consequences, shame, and guilt do not proceed from a heart that truly hates the first inroads of sin. Such people may not be "faking it" but may even believe that they truly hate sin as sin and can give the right answers about it.

The holiness we possess as Christians remains in a certain sense perfect in this life, but even this must be carefully explained. Sedgwick distinguishes between a perfection of integrity, which we possess, versus a perfection of eminency, which we do not possess. The former is a result of a holy heart that genuinely stands in opposition to hypocrisy; the latter consists in a complete opposition to all lusts. True Christians are not hypocrites like the Pharisees described in Matthew 23 because we possess the perfection of integrity: we are genuinely saved to a real holiness. But the grace we possess is still grace in a diseased soul that has darkness (i.e., indwelling sin) left in it.[11]

As Christians we are not perfect, but there is a sense in which we may be outwardly above reproach. This is actually a qualification for elders: "Therefore an overseer must be above reproach ... sober-minded, self-controlled, respectable, hospitable ... not a drunkard, not violent but gentle, not quarrelsome, not a lover of money" (1 Tim. 3:2–3). We do commit actual sins, but not to the degree we may have committed actual sins if we were converted later in life, for example. One can discern clear patterns of outward behavior of change in many who were converted in the adult years. But what all Christians, including those who are above reproach, will lament are the inward abominations that rise up all too often in their hearts. We are appalled at our secret sins.

None of us in this life escapes the revolting imaginations that arise in our hearts, even in the midst of prayer or corporate worship. We know when we are singing but not really paying attention to the words.

We are in public, singing beautiful hymns, but our hearts drift and wander. No one knows besides us and God. Sedgwick says, "Beloved the main battle of a Christian is not in the open field; his quarrels are most within, and his enemies are in his own breast, when he has reformed an ill life, yet it shall cost him infinitely much more to reform an ill heart."[12] Reforming our outward conduct, such as giving up foul language, is easy compared to reforming our hearts through the means appointed by God. The difficulty of the battle is mainly the battle within that we alone know of.

HYPOCRISY

Secret sins may be serious aggravations against God. Hidden from the public, but perhaps committed with another person with a degree of privacy, they can be some of the most heinous. Falsifying records, taxes, grades, etc., can lead to all sorts of grievous evils. Fornication, whether heterosexual or homosexual, is often in private between two or more individuals who seem to think a holy God is on vacation from their presence. Plenty of well-dressed businessmen in suits can be found visiting brothels and maintaining an apparently well-ordered family life, while their wives and children are unaware of dad's perversions going on in secret. This is hypocrisy, and it is hard to discern. As John Milton wrote in *Paradise Lost* (Book III, 684):

> For neither Man nor Angel can discern
> Hypocrisy, the only evil that walks
> Invisible, except to God alone.[13]

Our sins are not the result of some purely external force, but begin within. There are in every person the natural motions of the heart: "For from within, out of the heart of man, come evil thoughts, sexual immorality, theft, murder, adultery, coveting, wickedness, deceit, sensuality, envy, slander, pride, foolishness. All these evil things come from within, and they defile a person" (Mark 7:21–23). Sedgwick observed, "The nature which tempts you, that nature is in you, it is the womb of many and infinite sinful corruptions, and imaginations: it casts out wickedness as the fountain casts out water."[14] The world and the devil bring temptations, but even if there were not a world and a devil, we would all have a natural fire of inward temptations to keep us busy.

All are by nature born hypocrites. "There is a high depth of hypocrisy in the souls of men," argued Sedgwick, "whose proper work is to have a secret way contrary to an open profession." But there are different types of hypocrites. This means we cannot simply say "we are all hypocrites," and include both Christians and non-Christians in that statement.

There are three types of hypocrites: (1) natural hypocrisy, which affects every human heart, and is on display in every natural person; (2) soul-destroying religious hypocrisy, which speaks to those who put on a good show outwardly but inwardly hate all forms of true holiness; and (3) occasional hypocrisy, which applies to Christians who are not unsaved hypocrites like the Pharisees but can act inconsistently to their confession from time to time.

Christians must be on guard against hypocrisy. We do not realize the extent to which we refrain from sinning simply because we want man to think well of us instead of God. Now, there is nothing necessarily wrong with wanting man to think well of us if we are living for God's glory and acting in accordance with His law. But the danger comes when man's approval all but erases God's. Sedgwick offers this test: "Now try yourselves in this: what is the restraint of your sinning? Suppose all men in the world were in a dead sleep. Suppose that no eye did see you, suppose that no tongue of human justice would call you to account: would not your heart then with full sail spread out itself? Would you not now, like the lions in the night, wander about for your preys? Would not your heart turn out itself, let go itself, drive out its secret inclinations? Would you not do that in any place which you now commit in secret corners?"[15]

These are valuable questions. For hypocrites, what they do or think in private would be openly committed if the world were in a "dead sleep." They are held back in their abominations by their love of the glory that comes from man, but if that restraining influence were gone, then what would be left to keep them from sinning?

APPLICATION

The study of God's attributes is not only meant for theologians, pastors, and seminary students. The knowledge of God is eternal life (John 17:3). There is a good reason God is constantly affirming throughout His Word that He knows all and sees all. He is the omniscient, omnipresent God who does not miss a thing; nor is He ever indifferent to any act committed in His universe.

Our remaining indwelling sin wants to make practical atheists out of us so that we live as though God did not exist. But the Holy Spirit will remind us, in connection with God's Word, that not only does He know all and see all, but the triune God dwells in our hearts (Rom. 8:9; Eph. 3:17; 1 John 3:24). This is a special, covenantal indwelling whereby God identifies with us Himself.

Our secret sins are, in a certain sense, worse than those of a non-Christian. This is because we have the power to resist sin and the knowledge that we commit our evil thoughts and actions while in union with Christ. But, at the same time, we can ask God to mold our thoughts and private lives in accordance with His will and for His glory, knowing that He will give to us if we ask. Likewise, and this must never be regarded as a license for sin, this Savior will not abandon us but in grace cleanses and transforms us.

Moreover, awareness of secret sins reminds us of the glory of justification by faith alone. Some are more concerned about "justification by man alone," but when we seriously consider secret sins as well as public sins, we are left undone before God. Justification has to be by faith alone since we have so many private sins besides our public ones that it would be insanity to think we could stand before God in ourselves with a clear conscience.

Presbyterian minister from the late eighteenth and early nineteenth centuries, Samuel Stanhope Smith (1751–1819), once preached a sermon on hidden sins and asked,

> How many sins have escaped our knowledge or observation, even in the moment of committing them? How many upon a review of life, have escaped our recollection? How many have been covered by the deceitfulness of self-love? How many have . . . been mistaken for virtues, through the effect of false principles! Ah! *Who can understand his [errors]? We are altogether as an unclean thing! Our iniquities, like the wind, have taken us away! Cleanse us, O Lord, from secret faults!*[16]

Truly. Father, cleanse us from our secret faults, and justify us through Christ alone for the many faults that we are unaware of.

SIN'S PRESUMPTION: HIGHWAY TO HELL

NONE EXEMPT

There are a number of ways to look at sin. Is it open or hidden? Is it a greater or lesser sin? Is it done in ignorance or with a high-handed knowledge of what is wrong? With the latter act in mind, David prayed in Psalm 19:13,

> Keep back your servant also from presumptuous sins;
> let them not have dominion over me!
> Then I shall be blameless,
> and innocent of great transgression.

David prayed to be kept from committing presumptuous sins; not committing them will in turn make him blameless. Since original sin affects us all, we are all by nature prone to all sins. Original sin does not give us a break from certain sins, but the seed of every sin lurks in our heart, even if not acted upon. Though in Christ, Christians still possess remaining sin and are thus susceptible to all manner of sins, including presumptuous sins. David's request is not unique to him but remains one that all Christians should make before God on a regular basis. Many godly people have fallen victim to the sin of presumption, which is a warning to us all. None are entirely free from the guilt and danger of this type of sin. Such are exacerbated when they involve a professing Christian. The Christian who sins presumptuously commits a willing provocation against God and expects a free return of mercy in exchange. Few sins are worse in the Christian life than presuming upon the grace of God.

PRESUMPTION

To be presumptuous is to knowingly and willingly violate a set boundary. Applying this to God's standards revealed in His Word, presumptuous sins simply involve any sin committed in willful violation of the standards we know quite well. Thomas Manton (1620–77) calls these sins of knowledge the "most dangerous" since there is so much contempt of God's law and His kindness; it is a sign that one loves sin as sin.[1]

As we consider God's law, each person is bound to it, whether in or outside of Christ. As we have seen, sin is the transgression of the law. According to Sedgwick, "The law of God is his revealed will, for doing or forbearing, and it is the rule of nature, and actions; whatsoever things stands in conformity to its good, and whatsoever varies or swerves from it, that same is sin."[2] Commonly, we speak of sins committed in two forms related to what we know as sin: (1) Ignorantly without conscious awareness of sin, or (2) Presumptuously or deliberately with such awareness. Such a contrast David sets forth in Psalm 19 as he prays for forgiveness for "hidden faults," or sins committed unintentionally (v. 12), then prays to be kept from "presumptuous sins" or those done intentionally.

Manton speaks of presumptuous sins as those "against light and knowledge, wittingly and willingly committed, with a full consent of will, carried on obstinately and proudly against God. They are usually such open and gross sins as are manifest; as whoring, gluttony, drunkenness, which are manifest even to natural conscience; or else are manifest by the common light of Christianity, as denying the faith; so that there is no doubt of the unlawfulness of the act done."[3] Similarly, Sedgwick offers a great, though sobering, definition of such sin: "Presumptuous sins are the bold darings, and proud adventurings of the heart upon things or ways known to be unlawful against express threatenings, either upon a false confidence, or upon contemptuous slighting, or desperate wilfulness."[4] The basic idea is simple: presumption is a knowing willingness to disobey God. For the Christian, this includes presuming upon the grace of God so that in the sin there is also the expectation of future mercy for the sin willingly committed.

A presumptuous sin requires an unholy boldness and proud willingness. On the other hand, a temptation is not usually quite as daring. Indeed, as Sedgwick wrote, "Temptation beats down the actual strength of grace resisting, but presumption tramples down the light of the word opposing; therefore presumptuous sinners are said to sin with an exalted, or high hand; the sinner does put aside God's will, and prefers his own." The contrast between unintentional and intentional sin is found in the book of Numbers:

> "*If one person sins unintentionally*, he shall offer a female goat a year old for a sin offering. . . . *But the person who does anything with a high hand*, whether he is native or a sojourner, reviles the LORD, and that person shall be cut off from among his people. Because he has despised the word of the LORD and has broken his commandment, that person shall be utterly cut off; his iniquity shall be on him." (Num. 15:27, 30–31, emphasis added)

Intentional, presumptuous sinners know what they are doing. They extinguish what they see clearly as the light of God's Word to deliberately walk in darkness. Now, a truly presumptuous sin involves real knowledge of the wrong and a desire to do it. But, in the case of Christians, who possess the Spirit, there should always be apprehension in committing a high-handed intentional sin against God's express commandments. Such should assist in keeping the believer from sinning, but sadly this is not always the case. Sometimes, the trepidation and reticence may be extremely weak, but it should always be there to some degree. This is to say, sins of presumption can be carried out not only by unbelievers with some natural knowledge of what is right and wrong, but also by Christians with supernatural knowledge (i.e., the Scriptures) of God's will.

God has not remained silent regarding the consequences of sin. He threatens even His own children and from the very beginning (Gen. 2:17). A sin of presumption occurs when someone sins even though aware of the penalty. Before God this is a very serious path to walk on. Imagine seeing a bridge that threatens to collapse if you walk on it. The presumptuous sinner is aware of the threat: "Do not walk on this bridge; it will collapse." But the presumption leads us onto the bridge, regardless of the danger and threat. God warns His own people to beware not to turn their heart from the Lord and serve false gods (Deut. 29:18). The one who does is a "root bearing poisonous and bitter fruit, one who, when he hears the words of this sworn covenant, blesses himself in his heart, saying, 'I shall be safe, though I walk in the stubbornness of my heart.' This will lead to the sweeping away of moist and dry alike" (Deut. 29:18–19).

In the New Testament, we see the same type of threat to those who forsake corporate worship: "[Do not neglect] to meet together, as is the habit of some, but [encourage] one another, and all the more as you see the Day drawing near. For if we go on sinning deliberately after receiving the knowledge of the truth, there no longer remains a sacrifice for sins, but a fearful expectation of judgment, and a fury of fire that will consume the adversaries" (Heb. 10:25–27).

Christians who sin presumptuously have a false confidence and both misunderstand and trivialize the mercy of God. They think they can willfully sin against God because He will be merciful and forgive them later. They abuse the mercy of God in Christ by their deliberate disobedience. The problem with this attitude cannot be overstated. This is precisely the type of person on the road to apostasy according to God's Word (Deut. 29:18–19; Heb. 10:25–27). This may be the person, then, who has embraced the mercy of God mentally but knows nothing of true heart religion. It is actually God's mercy in Christ that keeps us from presumptuous sins.

If professing Christians willfully sin against God's law but think God will no doubt be merciful in the future, they are also making the assumption that they will have the strength for future repentance. But, as Sedgwick duly notes, we have no guarantee of a "future" repentance for such: "All life has its limits from the Lord of life and death; he who sins today cannot be assured that he shall live till tomorrow. Now repentance is a work of this life; death binds us over to sentence, and then it is too late to return. And therefore, every presumptuous sinner adventures boldly upon that which cannot be his, beyond the time present."[5] Likewise, we cannot be sure that we will even desire such repentance but may find ourselves with a heart hardened in the rut of unrepentance. Also, we are sinning against God but presuming upon God to give us the grace of repentance for the sin we have committed. "Though our natural principles can give the wound," says Sedgwick, "yet they must be supernatural principles which give the cure: our own hearts can cause us to fall, but God's grace only is that which raises us."[6] Presumptuous sins are aggravated by the fact that the person we dishonor is the One we depend on to rescue us from the dishonor we willfully committed. The antinomian spirit of the present age may not even see a problem with this, but such thinking is a deadly poison.

The sin of presumption loses the assurance of God's grace in return. In the end, it forfeits, in unbelief, the promise of such grace eternally.

The Israelites learned this the hard way. They went into battle but not always with God. When they failed to obey Him, they could not be assured of His presence with them: "So I spoke to you, and you would not listen; but you rebelled against the command of the LORD and presumptuously went up into the hill country" (Deut. 1:43). Indeed, not only was God not with them but He was against them. If you march against the Lord, do not be surprised if He marches against you. There can only be one victor in such a battle.

HEINOUSNESS OF SIN

The sin of presumption is, according to Manton, "an implicit blasphemy" (Num. 15:30; Ezek. 20:27). He warned, "There is a blasphemy included in it, as if God were an ignorant God, and did not know [the sinner's] wickedness; or a careless God, that would not take notice of it; or an impotent God, that could not punish his rebellion; or an unjust God, that would not."[7] What are we saying about God and His majesty when we willfully sin against Him? What are we saying about His attributes? Presumptuous sins chop Him up into pieces and take His love, mercy, and grace away from His other attributes such as knowledge, justice, power, and holiness.

In the presumptuous sinner exists, added Manton, "the highest pride in it that a creature can be capable of."[8] David sinned presumptuously in the examples of Bathsheba and Uriah. He took for himself what did not belong to him in his act of adultery and murder. He knew taking another man's wife and then his life was evil, but his pride gave him what he would deny to other men. In so doing, David despised God's word (2 Sam. 12:9). His sin of pride, which manifested itself in adultery and murder, meant the sword would never depart from his house (v.10). Despising God, an act of pride, always has consequences, and they can involve great loss physically and/or spiritually, even when the Father disciplines His children in tender love.

The Christian spends much time in the Word of God and in corporate worship being fed by teachers of the Word. Christians receive truth upon truth from God. They move from immaturity to maturity in their knowledge of the Lord. They experience God's power and grace. Then, to willfully sin in presumption not only tramples these heavenly gifts but also despises the gracious Lord who gave them.

ENDANGERMENT IN THE HARDENED HEART

Willfully sinning against God has many dangers for the unconverted and the converted, though in different ways. For the unregenerate, the repetition of presumptuous sins further hardens the heart. Manton noted, "Every day they sin away their tenderness. Men grow wilful by frequent sinning, and their hearts become as hard as the highway by frequent treading upon it.... By every presumptuous sin they put a new difficulty in the way of their conversion."[9] In addition, the more one sins against the Lord, the more one will face the natural consequences of sin in this life. Also, such sin compounds the baggage of former sins for one later converted, in terms of the grief suffered by and harm inflicted on self and others. We are forgiven for our past sins, but the consequences remain. Sometimes such involve the horror of remembering what we did and whom we sinned against (e.g., as in fornication or abusive anger). Sometimes physical effects such as health issues or economic hardship may continue (e.g., as in alcohol addiction or the reckless pursuit of pleasure).

But after regeneration the danger of presumptuous sins heightens in a manner that should sober us. Sins of weakness and ignorance are one thing, especially when very little deliberation occurs. But plotting evil against a clear command of God will lead, in Manton's view, to a "sad breach between God and the soul, throwing us into the depths of fear and perplexed thoughts. They waste our comforts, [and] wound our consciences."[10] True Christians can never lose God's unconditional love, which concerns His eternal love of benevolence to His elect. But these presumptuous sinners may stir up God's displeasure with them, as in the case of David: "And when the mourning was over, David sent and brought her to his house, and she became his wife and bore him a son. But the thing that David had done displeased the Lord" (2 Sam. 11:27).

God holds His own to a higher standard. To whom much is given, much is required (Luke 12:48). Because we have greater knowledge and greater powers to resist sin, our Lord may punish our sins of presumption in this life with a greater severity than He seems to inflict upon the ungodly. So, in Amos 3:2, we read of not only God's love for His people, but also His chastisement:

> "You only have I known
>   of all the families of the earth;
> therefore I will punish you
>   for all your iniquities."

Both David and Eli, along with their households, bore great consequences for their presumptuous sins. Speaking of Eli's toleration of his and his family's sins, Manton observed, "[Eli's] sons are slain in battle, Israel discomfited, the ark of God taken, Eli broke his neck, his daughter died in child-bearing, his house rejected, 1 Sam. 2:30. The anger of the Lord is very hot when we provoke him by these kind of sins; the revenging hand of God will lie very heavy on our persons, children, estate, and all other outward comforts. It is not safe to offend him."[11]

In the end, we are called to live for God's glory, and sinning presumptuously does the opposite. Such a life takes the name of the Lord in vain as we sin against Him willfully. We make our name superior to His by our actions and invite His displeasure. We harm ourselves and others by denying the dangerous consequences of presuming upon the Lord's grace.

APPLICATION

Sometimes we willingly enter a course of sinning and think that we shall, as Manton noted, "make amends for a course of sin in one kind by abounding in other duties; as some that live in uncleanness will be charitable, to excuse or expiate for the offences of a filthy life."[12] An accountant may knowingly cheat (rob) his clients for a huge sum of money but make a nice contribution to the church to "make up" for it. A woman may cheat on her husband but still aim to raise her children well. A child may steal from his parents but work hard at school. We often work hard in one area so that we can feel less guilty about a sin in another area. Presumptuous sin is deceitful, not just dangerous.

Consider three scenarios of someone driving: an electrician who sometimes stops for a few beers with his buddies and thinks nothing of getting behind the wheel over the legal limit; a young web designer who stays up late gaming and usually fights nodding off during his morning commute; and a physical therapist traveling to her home appointments habitually with her smartphone out and in use even for texting. Are any of these better than the others? All three constitute unfocused, impaired, illegal, and dangerous driving. All three people break the sixth commandment by disregard for the lives of themselves and others. Beyond this, they do it "all the time" and think that they, unlike others, are capable of staying safe. This is not skilled confidence but presumptuous pride. They know it's wrong, yet they keep on doing it, in spite of the close calls they have had. They are also presuming upon God's providence and mercy to keep them safe, even if they should make a mistake. *This day will be like any other,* they think. *Still, I need to stop doing this, it's madness,* they say to themselves. The time may never or too late come. What is the solution for presumptuous sinners as we all can be?

We cannot put sin to death, or think we are doing so, while we nurture our precious pet sin(s), stroked like Gollum's ring. We play with fire by indulging in something we know is wrong before the face of God. "I'll deal with it later," we insist, but the more we settle into the rut of this sin, the less likely we will ever deal with it. Owen perceptively states the "custom of sinning takes away the *sense* of it; the course of the world takes away the *shame* of it; and love to it makes men greedy in the pursuit of it."[13]

So, we must repent early and often. Presumptuous sins particularly grieve the Holy Spirit, God Himself, and dampen the power of His work in us. Let us then pray, as David did,

> Keep back your servant also from presumptuous sins;
>> let them not have dominion over me!
> Then I shall be blameless,
>> and innocent of great transgression. (Ps. 19:13)

SIN'S PRIDE: STAND TALL

FROM HEAVEN

After unbelief, nothing is more harmful to the soul than the sin of pride. In fact, in studies dating back to the fourth century and later popularized in the medieval church, the so-called seven deadly sins found their root in the sin of pride. These studies actually began, as Rebecca DeYoung notes, with a focus on the "seven capital vices," or the chief sins out of which other sins came to life like branches bearing "toxic fruit" and fed by the main-branch capital vices. The seven commonly observed include vainglory, envy, sloth, avarice (greed), wrath, lust, and gluttony. Like unbelief, pride is included in these seven sins.[1]

Satan's first sin was likely that of pride (1 Tim. 3:6). As the friend and associate of Charles Spurgeon, Archibald G. Brown, proclaimed in a sermon, "Perdition was prepared for the Devil and his angels, and pride prepared the Devil and his angels for perdition. We need fear no language we can possibly use being too strong to denounce pride."[2] Pride is a monstrous evil, containing all sins in it. Brown added, "The proud man is simply one who bends the knee and worships a more hateful idol than can ever be found in the whole catalogue of heathendom, and its name is 'Self!'"[3] This idolatry of self puts the sinner in competition with almighty God (Gen. 3:5). In such a contest, only God can emerge as the winner; but, against all reason, the proud continue their assault upon the omnipotent One.

Pride infects not just individuals but also groups, as in the famous Tower of Babel incident. The inhabitants of Shinar said, "Come, let us build ourselves a city and a tower with its top in the heavens, and let us make a name for ourselves, lest we be dispersed over the face of the whole earth" (Gen. 11:4). Pride overcomes not just "self" but "ourselves," not just a person but also a people. We all by nature want what only belongs to God: preeminence in all things. Instead of "Hallowed be your name," pride demands, "Hallowed be my name." Note that being a theist does not necessarily free someone from pride, for people, while believing in God, may put themselves before Him, leaving Him in second place. This constitutes self-worship, a violation of the first three commandments. Self and sin are practically synonymous for the natural man. All of the violations of God's commandments are expressions, in one way or another, of pride.

Whomever we encounter, whether in the mirror, or elsewhere, we can easily see the truth of Shakespeare's description of one of his characters:

> "but I can see his pride
> Peep through each part of him. Whence has he that,
> If not from hell?" [King Henry the Eighth, 1.1]

Pride peeps through every part of our being. The sweat off a person in a sauna is like the pride that flows from us. But while, like Shakespeare, we might be tempted to think pride came from hell, the story is quite different. Richard Newton (1840–1914) once said the history of pride can be summed up in three small chapters: "The beginning of pride was in heaven. The continuance of pride is on earth. The end of pride is in hell. This history shows how unprofitable it is."[4] What a frightening thing pride shows itself to be coming from heaven and ending up in hell, but not only through the fallen angels but also humanity. If unbelief is the foundation of the road to hell, then pride is the pavement that leads its offspring there.

GOD HATES PRIDE

We do not like to think about things God hates. We much prefer to dwell upon what and whom He loves. Dwelling on the latter can be an extraordinarily helpful spiritual discipline (if done biblically), whether in worship, prayer, song, or meditation. But how often do we meditate upon what God hates? How often do we sing about what God hates? Should we not be concerned to worship God for His whole being, including His attitude toward the universe He created? In other words, we have to give attention to not only what God loves but also what He hates. Our attitude toward pride should not be different from God's toward the arrogant, proud, and haughty. Regarding the proud, the Scriptures are clear:

> There are six things that the LORD hates,
>   seven that are an abomination to him:
> haughty eyes, a lying tongue,
>   and hands that shed innocent blood. (Prov. 6:16–17)

> "The fear of the LORD is hatred of evil.
> Pride and arrogance and the way of evil
>   and perverted speech I hate." (Prov. 8:13)

> Therefore it says, "God opposes the proud but gives grace to the humble." (James 4:6)

Why does God hate pride so much? Because His majesty can have no competition. He looks down upon such insignificant specks of dust and ashes (Gen. 18:27) and, with His infinitely accurate penetrating eye, beholds our desire to dethrone Him. Can He be indifferent to such madness?

Consider Sennacherib, the king of Assyria, who warned Hezekiah, king of Judah, not to trust in his God. Sennacherib claimed it was a farce if Hezekiah believed the Lord would protect Judah. After all, Sennacherib already wielded superiority over other kings and nations and their gods (2 Kings 19:10–13), and Hezekiah and Judah would be like them. Yet Sennacherib never did battle with the Lord of Hosts, who took note of Sennacherib's pride. After Hezekiah the king and Isaiah the prophet prayed to God, "the LORD sent an angel, who cut off all the mighty warriors and commanders and officers in the camp of the king of Assyria. So he returned with shame of face to his own land. And when he came into the house of his god, some of his own sons struck him down there with the sword" (2 Chron. 32:21).

God also did not look away from the pride of Sodom: "Behold, this was the guilt of your sister Sodom: she and her daughters had pride, excess of food, and prosperous ease, but did not aid the poor and needy" (Ezek. 16:49). As a result, "the LORD rained on Sodom and Gomorrah sulfur and fire from the LORD out of heaven" (Gen. 19:24). God destroyed Sodom not just because of the sexual perversions there, but the pride at the heart of such wickedness.

Whether King Nebuchadnezzar (Dan. 4:28–33) or Miriam (Num. 12) or King Uzziah (2 Chron. 26:16) or Herod (Acts 12:21–23), we see time and time again God's judgment on the proud.

CAUSES OF PRIDE

What enables the sin of pride to flower? There are many hindrances to humility or pathways to pride. For one, ignorance gives rise to pride.

In fact, ignorance of one's own ignorance explains a great deal about pride in this world. People do not really know who they are and who God is. Indeed, John Calvin famously began his *Institutes of Christian Religion* simply enough, but breathtakingly and profoundly: "Nearly all the wisdom we possess, that is to say, true and sound wisdom, consists of two parts: the knowledge of God and of ourselves."[5] In ignorance of self and God, we manifest ourselves as monstrous creatures, walking as children of the devil, puffed up with pride and an insane view of our pretended majesty. When people are converted, they not only put their faith in Jesus, but also experience a true spiritual humbling before God. In other words, in their loving embrace of the Savior, they repent, hating their sins in recognition of their moral perversity before a thrice holy God.

The doctrine of justification by faith alone, whereby we not only receive forgiveness of sins, but also the imputed righteousness of Christ, humbles us as it teaches us that we bring absolutely nothing to offer God in our salvation. We come to the Savior essentially proclaiming, "I'm a poor sinner and nothing at all, but Jesus Christ is my all in all; My hope is built on nothing less than Jesus' blood and righteousness." If we truly believe this glorious Protestant doctrine, there can be no room for pride in the Christian life. The step into Christ out of self is a step from pride to humility. Failure to grasp our utter moral bankruptcy is a major cause of pride in the natural man. He vainly believes he's not as bad as most and a great deal better than he really is. Ignorance can result from pride, but also be the cause of pride.

Pride also manifests itself through ignorance of the true and living God. Pride shrieks in horror at the thought of God's majesty and glory. Pride means a sinner would rather ascribe glory to images such as birds and animals than to God (Rom. 1:23), thus worshiping the creature rather than the Creator (Rom. 1:25). So, naturally, God judges idolatrous and boastful proud people (Rom. 1:30) by giving them up to their shameful passions (Rom. 1:26).

PRIDE'S FACE

Prideful ignorance of self and God leads to a whole host of problems. The proud are hell-bent upon doing their own will alone, often with hypocritical modesty. They also master the art of blame shifting and esteem their own gifts as better and more illustrious than those of others. The proud justify themselves continually but condemn others with consummate ease. They insist upon one law for themselves and another for others, with the latter being a great deal stricter than the former.

The proud think they are clever, and sometimes they even are! Pride tries to conceal itself under the pretense of genuine humility. Pride can show itself in nonverbal communication, simply by the eyes (Prov. 21:4) or by the manner of one's strut. Sometimes you see pride immediately by the tone and language of a person, but in others it can take years to manifest itself.

Those who are easily offended often struggle with pride; they take themselves too seriously and struggle to laugh at their deficiencies. The proud do not easily forgive others. They have failed to understand that their smallest sin against God is far worse than the biggest sin against them.

Pride has its omissions as well, such as an aversion to asking questions, seeking help, reading instructions, or admitting weakness. Proud people scoff at the performance of menial tasks and pursue only the responsibilities that provide fertile soil for their ego. Pride, because it gives birth to so many other sins, and is so often commission and also omission, possesses a sort of ubiquity among humans. It is a restless evil, even when it is "resting."

Pride possesses a universal and omnivorous appetite, feasting on anything and everything. The drunkard looks for alcohol; the glutton looks for food; but pride is not limited by anything. Many sins require a context and matter (e.g., food, alcohol, sex), but pride requires little to no help from the material world. It exercises itself in secret and in public; it shows itself in what it does and doesn't do; it sometimes boasts and then brags that it doesn't; it takes every and any situation and sizes it up for personal advantage.

C. S. Lewis called pride the "essential vice, the utmost evil. . . . Unchastity, anger, greed, drunkenness, and all that, are mere fleabites in comparison: it was through Pride that the devil became the devil: Pride leads to every other vice: it is the complete anti-God state of mind."[6] When Paul described false teachers, he referred to them as primarily proud people. They are "puffed up with conceit" (1 Tim. 6:4). This pride leads to "an unhealthy craving for controversy and for quarrels about words, which produce envy, dissension, slander, evil suspicions, and constant friction among people who are depraved in mind and deprived of the truth, imagining that godliness is a means of gain" (1 Tim. 6:4–5). Pride is the opposite of humility.

Pride is not only the opposite of humility but also of love. In 1 Corinthians 13:4–7, Paul described love as "patient and kind; love does not envy or boast; it is not arrogant or rude. It does not insist on its own way; it is not irritable or resentful; it does not rejoice at wrongdoing, but rejoices with the truth. Love bears all things, believes all things, hopes all things, endures all things." Conversely, pride wants immediate gratification; pride always envies and continually boasts. Pride is arrogant and rude; it insists on its own way; it is irritable and resentful; it make exceptions for itself in terms of wrongdoing and only demands the truth when convenient. Pride does not bear with others and hopes only good for self; it does not endure the failings of others and is self-promoting.

As the "mother of hell," pride is, declares Watson, "a complicated evil . . . it is a spiritual drunkenness; it flies up as wine into the brain, and intoxicates it."[7] Archibald G. Brown likewise says, "No wretched drunkard reeling along the road is a more pitiable or disgusting sight than the man who is intoxicated into idiocy with the alcohol of his own accursed pride."[8] In short, if remaining pride is perpetual drunkenness, then we all are, in a sense, spiritual drunkards.

There can be no doubt about the power of pride. Its many forms mean it is the hardest sin to subdue, the most difficult to root out and put to death. As Benjamin Franklin said in his *Autobiography,* "In reality, there is, perhaps, no one of our natural passions so hard to subdue as *pride.* Disguise it, struggle with it, stifle it, mortify it as much as one pleases, it is still alive and will every now and then peep out and show itself; you will see it, perhaps, often in this history; for even if I could conceive that I had completely overcome it, I should probably be proud of my humility."[9] If Benjamin Franklin, hardly known as a Christian, can see such truths, how much more should the children of God in Christ? In our time, pride is seen as closer to a virtue than a vice, let alone a sin, but this is not the biblical view.

APPLICATION

We are told in 2 Chronicles 32:25 that "Hezekiah did not make return according to the benefit done to him, for his heart was proud. Therefore wrath came upon him and Judah and Jerusalem." As is so often the case, judgment follows pride:

> Pride goes before destruction,
> and a haughty spirit before a fall. (Prov. 16:18)

Yet, remarkably, Hezekiah "humbled himself for the pride of his heart, both he and the inhabitants of Jerusalem, so that the wrath of the LORD did not come upon them in the days of Hezekiah" (2 Chron. 32:26). A few points are worth considering here.

God's humbling work in our lives remains the antidote for pride. We may not like it when He disciplines us with His loving and fatherly chastisement, and such is often more painful (and lengthy) than we wish. Yet we learn humility in the brokenness our loving Father inflicts. Indeed, Scripture contains commands to humble ourselves (1 Peter 5:6), but we are naturally averse to such a pursuit. Attaining true humility is often only realistic when God squeezes us in His providence. God's wrath came upon Hezekiah and Jerusalem, but when they humbled themselves, the Lord relented in compassion. He loves humility so much that He is more than willing to bless when the first sparks of a humble and contrite spirit fly upward toward heaven.

God blesses the humble by exalting them: "Humble yourselves, therefore, under the mighty hand of God so that at the proper time he may exalt you" (1 Peter 5:6). Also, Matthew 23:12, "Whoever exalts himself will be humbled, and whoever humbles himself will be exalted." We see this in God's own pattern for Christ's life in Philippians 2:5–11. As our Savior, Christ willingly humbled Himself, and God willingly exalted Him. There is no way for the Christian in this life but "down," if we wish to be brought "up." Paul's own biography in the next chapter displays this movement. He was proud of his religious accomplishments (Phil. 3:4–7) at one time. But, by the grace of God, he counted everything as loss "because of the surpassing worth of knowing Christ Jesus my Lord. For his sake I have suffered the loss of all things and count them as rubbish, in order that I may gain Christ" (Phil. 3:8). Thus, by sharing in Christ's sufferings, Paul aimed to "attain the resurrection from the dead" (Phil. 3:11). The pattern for Paul, coming from a position of spiritual pride, was suffering, humility, and future exaltation. No Christian can escape this pattern that God has, in His wisdom, established: from high (pride) to low (humility) to high (God's exaltation). Let us who struggle with pride pursue humility in Christ, who humbled Himself for us to save us from the guilt and power of pride so that He may exalt us in due time.

SIN'S SELFISHNESS: ALL YOU NEED IS LOVE

GOD'S GIFTS RUINED

Some of the greatest gifts God gave to humanity in His wise, loving constitution of man and woman have been skewed horribly with the entrance of sin. Inherent to sin is the love of self, which can be a complex idea for Christians to understand. We are inundated constantly with worldly philosophies of self-advancement, self-esteem, self-fulfillment, self-actualization, and self-gratification. We see the potential or likely troubles in these ideas and run in the opposite direction, sometimes even believing that self-love is always or necessarily wrong.

Indeed, self-love in the natural man is, as Goodwin called it, "the viceroy, lord paramount in this kingdom of sin (for when God was deposed from being our utmost end, ourselves succeeded as next heirs)," He added that the chief principle

> which guides us in our actions . . . is self-love, and all the power and force that reason has is turned and bent to advance and set it up, to maintain and uphold its prerogative. And now, then, that self-love is made a man's utmost end, and is the lord

paramount and chief governor in this new erected kingdom of sin.[1]

In short, man dethroned God and we have seated ourselves in His place, where we seek to be lord. Self-love, then, overlaps significantly with the mutinous and deposing nature we observed in the last chapter concerning pride.

This gives the impression, then, that self-love is necessarily wrong. But this is where we have to be careful. Historically, Reformed theologians have spoken of three types of self-love. They distinguished between a natural self-love, which all creatures possess; sinful self-love, which all humans possess; and gracious self-love, which God's chosen ones possess.

NATURAL SELF-LOVE

By nature, to exist is to love oneself. This natural self-love is part of the law of nature, which even animals possess. To exist is, in one sense, to love oneself. According to Charnock, "This self-love is not only commendable, but necessary, as a rule to measure that duty we owe to our neighbor, whom we cannot love as ourselves, if we do not first love ourselves: God having planted this self-love in our nature, makes this natural principle the measure of our affection to all mankind of the same blood with ourselves."[2]

The person who eats and sleeps shows a form of self-love insofar as such acts are preserving life. Even non-Christians possess this type of self-love. Of course, with sin, people can and do show self-hate when they starve themselves or even indulge in such gross gluttony that they are destroying their bodies. Still, we should see that living life in some sense manifests self-love as does breathing air or drinking water to sustain life. Going to the doctor and taking medication for an illness are done out of self-love. When we laugh with friends or put on warm clothes on a cold day, we are showing self-love. Much self-love arises from a natural principle in all of us to rightfully preserve the quality of our life.

SINFUL SELF-LOVE

The self-love to be avoided is carnal self-love. This love arises in the human heart as naturally as we breathe. According to Charnock, such opposes God, "when our thoughts, affections, designs, centre only in our own fleshly interest, and rifle God of his honour. . . . Thus the natural self-love, in itself good, becomes criminal by the excess, when it would be superior and not subordinate to God."[3] Cowards, for example, are those who live according to sinful self-love; they do not live by faith and so they live in fear (Rev. 21:8).

Paul refers to sinful self-love when he speaks of the last days when people "will be lovers of self, lovers of money, proud, arrogant" (2 Tim. 3:2). Our thoughts, plans, desires, etc., all focus on our own fleshly interest. A good thing, love of self, becomes a bad thing because of sin. Sinful desires foster excess as our will and glory become superior to God's will (John 5:44). Sinful self-love actually manifests self-hatred, because so long as we are placing ourselves on God's throne, we abandon our best interests. This type of self-love (pride) hurts, destroys, kills, and leads to judgment. All sins are a result of this passion, or as Manton says, "the root of corruption is carnal self-love, for it is at the bottom of other sins; because men love themselves, and their flesh as themselves, more than God."[4]

We all have a number of self-love sins: self-pity, self-confidence, self-sufficiency, self-hate, self-will. Our anger usually arises because others are observing our mandate, "My will be done!" We envy because we want what someone else has. We lust, satisfying our internal illicit desires, often at the expense of someone else who did not (and likely would not) give us permission to ogle them in our heart, digitally, or otherwise. Laziness is a form of self-indulgence whereby we inordinately rest, sometimes at the expense of others who must now work harder. Impatience results, like anger, from our will not being accomplished as quickly as we would like. Greed seeks more for self than necessary. Like the Israelites vainly and wrongly scavenging for extra manna, we want tomorrow's bread (and that for the day after, and on and on) today. And pride pursues self-worth higher than we ought, usually thinking that we deserve more than the next person or that our gifts are more excellent than theirs are.

Charnock understood that "sin indeed may well be termed a man's self"; it is "the form that overspreads every part of our souls."[5] Often our idea of what is true and good is not God's Word, but "the inclinations of self, the gratifying of which is the aim of our whole lives."[6] We so often justify our acts as good out of self-love. Sin and self are the same for the natural man.

Self-love is idolatry. In fact, as Sibbes says, "he is the idol and the idolater; he has a high esteem of himself, and those that do not highly esteem him he swells against them."[7] This explains why true conversion must be a divine work. We love ourselves so much that our desire to relinquish our throne is nonexistent. Sometimes we hear from well-intentioned people, "Do you want to accept Jesus into your heart?" This is not a terrible question when we consider what such an invitation entails in the Lord's eyes. But true conversion happens when we willingly, albeit painfully, give up our throne, relinquish our will as absolute, and happily serve another's ways and desires, namely, Jesus the Lord of all. Speaking to the Jews, Jesus said: "How can you believe, when you receive glory from one another and do not seek the glory that comes from the only God?" (John 5:44).

Self-love implies self-applause. We need little assistance, though we welcome the reminders, to reflect upon our natural giftings or achievements in this world (see Eccl. 2:1–11). Paul warns the Romans not to think of themselves more highly than they ought (Rom. 12:3). Why does Paul have to say that? Because even Christians can be prone to such excess, often evidenced by our actions on social media. By nature, it is impossible to have an accurate view of ourselves. Charnock puts the matter well:

> Few think of themselves so [lowly] as they ought to think: this sticks as close to us as our skin; and as humility is the beauty of grace, [self-applause] is the filthiest soil of nature. Our thoughts run more delightfully upon the track of our own perfections than the excellency of God; and when we find anything of a seeming worth, that may make us glitter in the eyes of the world, how cheerfully do we grasp and embrace ourselves![8]

Hence we read of such a person, the Pharisee, who prayed: "God, I thank you that I am not like other men, extortioners, unjust, adulterers, or even like this tax collector" (Luke 18:11). The Pharisee aptly reflects the carnal self-love in all of our hearts by nature.

With sinful self-love, we wage war with God as we seek our own glory as our highest end rather than God's, which leads to all of our sins. God makes Himself His highest end as He loves Himself for His perfections, all He does, and all He refrains from doing. We are to adopt this view of God, namely, to think God's thoughts after Him. Instead, the natural man thinks his own thoughts of himself as he elevates himself to the place where God belongs.

The chief end of the natural man is to glorify himself and enjoy himself. Out of self-love, not only do we fail to love God as we ought but also our neighbor. As Goodwin argued, God subdues His enemies out of love for Himself (1 Cor. 15:24–28), while we wrongly strive to overpower others and "get the victory, and to keep ourselves uppermost."[9] This explains our ungodly quest for revenge.

In 1 Corinthians 13:4–5, Paul spoke of love as "patient and kind;

love does not envy or boast; it is not arrogant or rude. It does not insist on its own way; it is not irritable or resentful." "The opposite sins," Goodwin said, "to all these come from self-love, which is opposite to the love of God. And so you see that other ground of that branch of our lusts, inordinacy, that they are not carried only to other things besides God as the chief good, but also to things contrary to God and the good of others."[10] Sinful self-love is thus, first, against God, and, second, against our fellow man. What can cure this?

SUPERNATURAL SELF-LOVE

The cure for self-love is self-love. The good self-love we ought to attain to is what Charnock calls "a gracious self-love." Speaking of the three types of self-love, he explains: "The first is from nature, the second from sin, the third from grace. The first is implanted by creation, the second the fruit of corruption, the third is by the powerful operation of grace."[11] To truly love ourselves we must love ourselves as God wants. Additionally, He wants us to remember all of the promises He makes to those who love themselves on His terms.

When we do everything to the glory of God in Christ, we love ourselves rightly. We do so even more than the natural self-love that sustains life, because we are thinking of eternity and not just this present world. For example, in Matthew 16:24–25, our Lord says to His disciples, "If anyone would come after me, let him deny himself and take up his cross and follow me. For whoever would save his life will lose it, but whoever loses his life for my sake will find it." This is true self-love: to deny oneself—which is to relinquish sinful self-love—in order to gain one's life. Similarly, those who leave family for the sake of Christ "will receive a hundredfold and will inherit eternal life" (Matt. 19:29). Gracious self-love is living a life of self-denial as we serve Christ first and foremost and believe the promises that await the faithful. Sinful self-love wants to be first and have the priority, but as our Lord testifies,

"Many who are first will be last, and the last first" (Matt. 19:30).

Our Lord sets forth the preeminent example of gracious self-love. He truly practiced what He preached: "In all things I have shown you that by working hard in this way we must help the weak and remember the words of the Lord Jesus, how he himself said, 'It is more blessed to give than to receive'" (Acts 20:35). Here Paul highlighted the importance of gracious self-love when we help the weak, for, "It is more blessed to give than to receive." If we want the blessed life, we don't get it through carnal self-love but through gracious self-love whereby we love others and so receive our reward in the end.

Jesus also desired the love and approval of His Father, which He was only too pleased to publicly and privately offer His beloved Son. The Father loved Jesus because He willingly obeyed to the point of death: "For this reason the Father loves me, because I lay down my life that I may take it up again" (John 10:17). This, again, constitutes gracious self-love, namely, to receive the love of God the Father. How does our Lord receive such love? By giving up His life, He obeys the Father, saves His people, and receives the name above every name (Phil. 2:9–11).

Paul wrote of how and why a husband should love his wife in Ephesians 5:22–33. In verse 28, he explained how the man who loves his wife loves himself. This is gracious self-love. A husband who sacrifices for his wife truly loves himself. This may be applied to the Lord, the husband of His bride, the church. By loving us, He loves Himself. And by loving Himself, He loves us. The holy and pure self-love of Christ is the reason we have been saved from our sin. For this reason, we can say that no person on earth has ever loved himself as much as Jesus does. And for that we can be thankful that the solution to our sinful self-love is Jesus' sinless self-love, which we are to imitate in our Christian living. This love from above must be supernatural, because it goes against every fiber of our natural selves.

APPLICATION

God defeats death by death, namely, the death of His Son. God defeats laziness by telling us to rest in Him and also enjoy the Lord's Day rest as preparation for the six days of labor. In the same vein, God's Word shows us that a cure for self-love is self-love. We move from a sinful self-love to a gracious, supernatural self-love. In this manner, our Lord Jesus shows us the way of true self-love.

We often exhort people to "look to Christ." But what does this mean? In Hebrews 12:2, for example, it means we look to Jesus who, as the pioneer and perfecter of our faith, went to the cross with joy, knowing He would be vindicated and glorified by the Father. He was, as we have seen, showing true self-love. We can do difficult things in life by looking to Jesus and knowing that rewards are very often attached to the performance of difficult spiritual duties. To love ourselves truly and rightly, as difficult as that pursuit remains, we must embrace all of the promises God offers in His Word.

We also must continually meditate upon this truth, even as our hearts continually tell us otherwise: sinful self-love is actually self-hate. This requires faith, because we are so naturally inclined toward selfishness at the expense of God and our neighbor. Remember, when we sin, we really hate ourselves and, very often, others. When tempted to sin, we should say to ourselves, "Why would you hate yourself so much as to do that?" By God's grace and with our eyes of Jesus, we can say no and then aim to truly love ourselves by putting self down in order that God may lift us up in due time. Even as we take the Lord's Supper we are showing true love to self by looking at the love of Christ for His body.

12

SIN'S ENVY: HEY JEALOUSY

PAIN-INDUCING ENVY

Envy is the daughter of pride. Envy as a sin gives no satisfaction due to the pain it experiences at the good fortune of others. Envy stresses over someone else having what we don't or more than what we do. It clearly is not limited to material things, but often includes a good name or reputation that we wish were true of us, sometimes exclusively so. The sense of entitlement that plagues contemporary Western culture only intensifies the envy that already burns within us.

Envy causes a disruption between a person and that person's neighbor. Instead of joy and thanksgiving, envy brings distress over someone else's blessings in life. The envious person, perhaps in an indirect manner, despises the authority and providence who has chosen to bless others as He sees fit. When we want for ourselves what the Lord has chosen to give to someone else, our agitation declares, "God, You messed up. Let me tell You how to preserve and govern this world in a more holy and wise manner." In envy we hate God's wisdom, goodness, and mercy for the simple reason that we do not enjoy how we feel regarding others.

This inward desire of envy often lurks hidden from others and remains best known to the one poisoned by it. Many sins are visible by their act (e.g., murder), but envy allows us to smile at our neighbor, say "nice SUV you have there," but inwardly hate him for his car, house, wife, children, job, wealth, athletic ability, or whatever. It may well be that Satan was envious of Adam and Eve before they sinned. They had what he lost, and in his pride he sought to take away from them what he did not possess (e.g., true felicity). Perhaps John Milton was on to something in his epic, *Paradise Lost*, when he spoke of Satan's aims:

> Who first seduced them to that foul revolt?
> The infernal Serpent: he it was, whose guile,
> *Stirred up with envy* and revenge, deceived
> The mother of mankind . . . (Book I)[1]

Envy is a trademark of the wicked, whereby they seek to harm others in their unhappiness, especially those like themselves. At its core, envy attacks God and His sovereign control of all things. Envy wants to take the wheel from the Lord.

THE WICKED ENVY

The natural man readily displays envy from his heart, from which the Lord explains come all manner of sins: "For from within, out of the heart of man, come evil thoughts, sexual immorality, theft, murder, adultery, coveting, wickedness, deceit, sensuality, envy, slander, pride, foolishness" (Mark 7:21–22). Some of these sins are obviously linked with envy (e.g., theft, coveting). Paul wrote similarly of the wicked in Romans 1. They are "filled with all manner of unrighteousness, evil, covetousness, malice. They are full of envy, murder, strife, deceit, maliciousness . . ." (Rom. 1:29). Envy fills the natural man, so much so that other sins are the outflowing of it—even murder (see 1 Sam. 18;

2 Sam.15–19). The works of the flesh include envy; not only the sexually immoral, but the envious will not inherit the kingdom of God (Gal. 5:21). From the time of the ancient church, envy has commonly been listed as one of the seven capital sins, all of which arise out of pride. In fact, in a certain sense, envy "makes the world go 'round." The preacher said in Ecclesiastes 4:4, "Then I saw that all toil and all skill in work come from a man's envy of his neighbor. This also is vanity and a striving after wind." Cultures, communities, neighborhoods, etc., can be showcases of envy. Whether phones, houses, cars, boats, four-wheelers, vacations, or fame, "keeping up with the Joneses" is a phrase fueled by envy. Pride and envy work together to ensure that we always get more than the next guy.

GREAT UNHAPPINESS

Why does so much unhappiness exist in this world? It certainly comes because of sin, but we must look deeper into this human plight. We know that sin brings misery into this world and our lives, despite any number of temporal blessings we receive. Likewise, the godless do not look at the world through the eyes of God. They can never be satisfied, since they see life through a different lens than the Christian. Only the latter knows, while he struggles with it, that a good and gracious God controls all things in this world and in our lives as He moves all of history to its final end.

The Lord provides gifts to men, women, and children according to His wisdom, goodness, and power. He blessed Isaac "a hundred-fold" so that he "became rich, and gained more and more until he became very wealthy. He had possessions of flocks and herds and many servants, so that the Philistines envied him" (Gen. 26:12–14). The Philistines clearly did not enjoy the treatment Isaac received. He had what they wanted.

Similarly, a few chapters later in Genesis, we learn of Rachel's envy: "When Rachel saw that she bore Jacob no children, she envied her sister [Leah]. She said to Jacob, 'Give me children, or I shall die!'" (Gen. 30:1). Rachel's envy did not work out well for her. First, such is the nature of envy that it prompted her to make an unfair demand upon her husband. Second, she finally got her wish, but ended up dying (Gen. 35:16–19).

In Proverbs 14:30 we hear the basic point about the foolishness of envy, from the perspective of personal happiness: "A tranquil heart gives life to the flesh, but envy makes the bones rot." Indeed, this sin brings no enjoyment or satisfaction at all, but that does not keep us from committing it. Such is the madness of sin. Even for Christians, when we know the harmful nature of envy, we still get terribly agitated as we reflect upon the success of others, instead of holding a settled confidence in a God who knows what we do and do not need.

GREAT HARM

The problem with envy as a sin is not merely that it makes us unhappy. That would be bad enough. But our unhappiness over the (sometimes perceived) good that another has can lead to us harming our neighbor in a number of different ways.

The story of Saul and David in 1 Samuel is instructive concerning the danger of envy for all involved, both guilty and innocent. Like Isaac, David prospered; he was successful (1 Sam. 18:5, 14–15). Certainly, God had graciously granted this prosperity, but in part, David did well because he lived wisely. The Lord was clearly with David, as the text says (1 Sam. 18:12, 14, 28). Just as Joseph's brothers envied him and sought to destroy him, Saul wanted to destroy David out of envy. Saul clearly hated that people loved David, including Jonathan, his son. In fact, we read that Michal, Saul's daughter, loved David, giving us the only recorded instance in the Old Testament relating the love a woman had for a man (1 Sam. 18:20). Saul's servants spoke duplicitously to David on behalf of Saul, telling David that he would be Saul's son-in-law. David responded, acknowledging his little worth: "I am a poor man and have no reputation" (1 Sam. 18:23). However, David had more success than Saul's other servants, "so that his name was highly esteemed" (1 Sam. 18:30). Out of Saul's pride, his envy burned toward David, who succeeded because the Lord was with him. Envy so raged that Saul became obsessed with murdering David (1 Sam. 19).

The envier may not actually kill the envied, but the latter can be damaged in other ways such as in non-physical yet personal attacks on their character. Think of the "employee of the month" guy whom the boss praises and the other workers constantly malign (he supposedly makes them "look bad" with his diligent work ethic). Yet injuring others' reputations or rejoicing in their apparent misfortune never truly satisfies and certainly does not relieve envy. Also, those who envy fail to see how unskilled they are at interpreting God's providence. The adversity or "bad luck" suffered by the envied may be the means God uses to actually bless them in a way unknown to the envier. Just ask Joseph, whose brothers meant their treatment of him for "evil" while "God meant it for good" (Gen. 50:20). God easily overrules wicked schemes in the love He shows His people. No matter that the envier does all sorts of things to rectify the situation hatefully. The Lord can and often does make it backfire, as one who "digs a pit will fall into it, and a stone will come back on him who starts it rolling" (Prov. 26:27).

If we feel pain at someone else's success or blessing, we aim to use our own methods to make that person endure a bit of the pain we feel. We not only want their success, but we long for them to feel loss and pain. The envious person rejoices when someone else suffers loss; envy is anti-love.

WHOM WE ENVY

We do not immediately like people who are similar to us. This may sound odd, but a closer look reveals that we are often prone to envy them instead. While it is possible, musicians do not typically struggle with envy toward athletes, nor athletes toward teachers. We all possess certain gifts and callings and when individuals with the same ones enjoy success, envy swells up in us like a balloon.

The Jewish religious leaders, the chief priests and elders, envied Jesus. Even godless Pilate could sense this: "For [Pilate] knew that it was out of envy that they had delivered him up" (Matt. 27:18). The envy in the hearts of the wicked religious leaders caused them to inflict harm on Jesus. But it was also because Jesus was a true religious leader, one whom God was with in His ministry. In our times, pastoral envy can be a serious problem, whether it is pain over reputation or distress over the size of a congregation. Yet a pastor usually does not struggle in the same ways with envy concerning a person in a completely different field who enjoys a great reputation as a botanist, for example. Envy plagues all of us, but it is often exacerbated when we compare ourselves to people like ourselves, especially those we think we surpass in gifts and abilities.

Social media adds to this problem. It creates an imbalanced perspective of the world and of others' lives. We typically see people at their best and happiest, portrayed on a screen that often posts the best picture (possibly even Photoshopped) out of one hundred. We see the highs of their lives, but rarely do we see the lows. We begin to envy what others have and live our lives as voyeurs. No wonder studies consistently show that excessive use of social media can add to depression or even cause it. How many times have we spent an hour or so on Facebook to "catch up" on our "friends" and come away feeling discouraged about our lives and how we need something more, something like they have? In other words, we sinfully let envy reign in a partially fake online world nurtured by the tech giants. So besides being an unenjoyable sin, we make it worse by thinking others are doing a lot better than we are when this is not necessarily the case.

Some of what we see on social media seems to involve depressed people looking at other depressed people all under the guise of happiness. It is envy that robs us of true happiness and offers instead real depression.

WHY WE ENVY

There are many reasons why we envy. Usually in our dissection of sin, we should consider how it occurs primarily against God. Envy is no different. For example, consider how envy rebels against God's sovereignty. His providence, and how He governs all things in the world, is mysterious and beyond our ability to comprehend. This should humble us when it comes to the affairs of the world and specifically how it extends to us individually. We see things with a limited perspective, with jaundiced eyes even in a state of grace. We often interpret events incorrectly. Envy fails to love and embrace God's providential rule in this world.

Envy is also silly because the Lord may give something to someone, and that apparent gift may end up being to their detriment. For example, someone's popularity, which we want for ourselves instead, may facilitate that person's falling into scandalous sin. How badly do we want what they have? Would we insist that things would be different for us? Worse yet, would we, in connection with our envy, delight in such a fall? Or we may be unhappy at the blessing another possesses and wish that for ourselves, not knowing that if it was ours, we would not handle it well. Some seem to be able to manage good looks or great prestige, but it may be a curse for others. In short, we must not imagine for a second that we could properly handle the gifts others receive. Perhaps instead of pain over what others have, we should feel some relief and satisfaction that God knows what and how much to give us as well as others.

If we truly believe that the Lord is good, wise, powerful, and sovereign, we have no grounds for envy. The statements "God is good" and "God will provide" mean we do not need to be envious of others. He gives to some what He denies to others. We must be content with that. True, we may wish to emulate what we see in others. But this means we cannot feel pain at their blessing. Once we resent others for what they have that we do not possess, we are being envious. And envy will not solve our problems but only add to them.

The Christian can turn to God's promise in Romans 8:28 and remember that, because we love God (because He first loved us!), all things are working together for our good. This is a powerful antidote to envy, namely, to believe God's promises rather than lusting after things others have.

There are other reasons for envy too. Harvey Newcomb (1803–63), a nineteenth-century American preacher and writer, made four points about envy. First, envious people lack self-respect. He wrote: "If we respect ourselves, we shall not desire the hollow importance arising from wealth, so much as to grieve that others have more of it than ourselves; nor shall we be willing to concede so much merit to the possession of wealth, as to suspect those who have it of esteeming us the less because we have it not."[2]

Second, an envious person lacks a generous spirit or goodwill toward others that rejoices in their success. Newcomb says, "The truly benevolent mind desires the increase of rational enjoyment, and will therefore rejoice in the happiness of others, without respect to his own."[3]

Third, one lacking magnanimity or an altruistic spirit is usually beset by envy. In fact, as Newcomb suggests, "The truly great will rejoice in the intellectual and moral elevation of others, as adding so much to the sum of human excellence. But the envious person cannot bear to see any other one elevated above himself. This is the spirit that brought Haman to the gallows; and Satan from the seat of an archangel to the throne of devils."[4]

Fourth, an envious person is, at bottom, a selfish person: "The law of God requires us to love our neighbor as ourselves.... But the envious person will hate his neighbor, because he is not permitted to love him less than himself."[5]

When you consider these reasons that we envy, no wonder we have such little happiness or peace. As Newcomb rightly recognizes, the "envenomed darts" of envy "will rankle and corrode in your bosom, and poison all your enjoyments. It is a disposition which can never be satisfied, so long as there is a superior being in the universe. It is aimed ultimately at the throne of God; and the envious person can never be happy while God reigns."[6]

APPLICATION

Christians can combat envy in a number of ways. However, we can ask two things of God in the mortification of envy and its replacement with something better. This is necessarily the goal of Christian sanctification in terms of dealing with sin: we put off our sin and put on righteous behavior (Eph. 4:22–32).

First, we can ask God for true happiness. Envy makes us miserable. And no one truly wants to be miserable. So as we have had our eyes open to the foolishness of envy we can ask God to give us true joy, blessedness, and delight. In Psalm 4:6–7 we read:

> There are many who say, "Who will show us some good?
>   Lift up the light of your face upon us, O LORD!"
> You have put more joy in my heart
>   than they have when their grain and wine abound.

Only God can give us true joy. Living in His presence, knowing that He is pleased with us, helps us to remain content in every and any circumstance (Phil. 4:11–12). If we can do all things through Christ who strengthens us (Phil. 4:13), we can experience joy instead of envy for others when we see them blessed. Those who set their minds on things above (Col. 3:2) will be able to resist the urge to think their happiness comes from having what others possess.

Second, we can ask God for true love toward not only Him but also our neighbor. Love does not envy (1 Cor. 13:4). Love rejoices at others being more prosperous, intelligent, or successful. Maybe we are spurred on to be better ourselves as we look at others and their enjoyments, but love keeps us from envying. If we envy that person, we hate (not love) them in our hearts, despite what we say with our mouths. The more we experience the love of Christ and, in turn, love others as He did, the more we shall be free from envy. What will this look like? Watson drew us a picture of the person who is mortifying envy: "A humble man studies his infirmities and another's excellencies, and that makes him put a higher value upon others than himself."[7]

Love begets humility and humility wishes well to others instead of harm. In so doing, we can feel joy instead of pain at the good that others possess. At the same time, we will feel their pain, truly, in the losses they experience, as we learn more and more, by God's grace to "rejoice with those who rejoice" and "weep with those who weep" (Rom. 12:15).

SIN'S UNBELIEF: LOSING MY RELIGION

FIRST THE WORST

There is no more harmful sin in the world than that of unbelief. Thomas Goodwin wrote: "Unbelief was the chief of man's first sin. Their first miscarrying was not believing God's word, and therefore they especially wounded our nature with unbelief; and faith being extinguished, the contrary principles have come to possess the mind."[1] This is the sum and substance of our problem as humans.

Likewise, Charnock, in his penetrating and soul-searching discourse on the sin of unbelief, referred to it as the "fountain of all sin. It was the first sin of Adam. . . . It was the cause also of all the sin that grew up to such maturity in the old world. . . . The faith of Abel is applauded (Heb. 11:4); consequently, the unbelief of Cain, the head of the wicked world, is marked. If Abel's sacrifice was more excellent in regard of his faith, Cain's was more vile in regard of his unbelief."[2]

The eternal destiny of all people may be summed up in Christ's words in John 8:24, "For unless you believe that I am he you will die in your sins." When faith replaces unbelief, all sins committed vanish; but if unbelief remains, there will one day be a "public explosion" of all our sins at the final judgment. One may only enter heaven through faith, as well as hell through unbelief. They are "tickets" to their respective destinations.

God gives His best, the Son and the Spirit, to overcome the worst, our unbelief. The Spirit grants us faith, not simply in God but in Jesus Christ, the mediator between God and man (1 Tim. 2:5). This occurs as the Spirit breathes new life into us, in accordance with the Father's will, in order that we may believe in His only begotten Son (John 3:16; 14:1). The poison of unbelief requires the best medicine that God can offer, namely, the two greatest gifts He could possibly give in His Son and our faith. The glory of the solution manifests the heinousness of the sin. The terrible nature of unbelief shows itself through the powerful blinding nature of sin and the work of the devil upon unbelievers. Unbelief is not merely intellectual but involves a radical sin problem.

UNBELIEVERS' UNBELIEF

There exist two main types of unbelief among the faithless. First, "negative unbelief" (*carentia simplex fidei*) refers to those never hearing the gospel of Christ explicitly, perhaps with no knowledge of it at all, and has been historically attributed to the so-called heathen. Second, "privative unbelief" (*carentia fidei debitae inesse*) refers to those hearing the gospel while refusing to believe on Christ as Savior. The former stand guilty before God but without being charged for rejecting the gospel (Rom. 1:20). The latter are charged with the more serious sin of consciously rejecting the good news (John 3:16–18).

Those in the first category of unbelievers are charged with what has been called "material infidelity." They cannot believe the good news when they are ignorant of it, yet they still bear responsibility for their lack of faith (infidelity). Following from this, unbelievers hearing the gospel, at least in its essence, are charged with "formal infidelity."

We can therefore understand Christ's words in John 15:22 in light of this distinction: "If I had not come and spoken to them, they would not have been guilty of sin, but now they have no excuse for their sin." Jesus is not saying that they have no guilt, but that His coming for and revealing of God's saving purposes makes the rejecters of such specifically guilty. In the same way, Jesus denounced Chorazin and Bethsaida because He had done mighty works there and they would not repent and believe. If these works had been done in the Gentile cities of Tyre and Sidon, they would have repented "in sackcloth and ashes" (Matt. 11:20–21). The "formal infidelity" of Chorazin and Bethsaida receives a more severe judgment than the "material infidelity" of Sodom (Matt. 11:24). To whom much is given much is expected (Luke 12:48).

TYPES OF UNBELIEVERS

Many have heard, studied, and evaluated the gospel only to ridicule it. From Julian the Apostate to Bertrand Russell, there are no shortage of examples of people knowingly and willingly rejecting the good news from God. Both our Lord and the apostle Paul clearly agonized over such open denial by the Jewish people in their day.

Some have even experienced what we may call a superficial attraction or an initial "awakening" through a pricked conscience and an attraction to gospel truth. In the end, something happens that turns the person away from such initial stirrings, perhaps because of fleshly desires, worldly counsel, mistreatment by professing Christians, or a direct attack of the evil one. Regarding such schemes of the devil, Charnock notes, "The first temptation Satan assaults the soul with, after some awakenings of conscience, is to question the matter to be believed. If he can hinder men from laying the foundation of truth in their understanding, he prevents all the superstructure, which cannot be raised without it."[3]

Others do not vigorously oppose the gospel, but express respectful disagreement through doubts or skepticism that keeps them from assenting to the good news. They may even say, "I would like to believe it is true, but its claims are implausible." While such are not proud atheists, they still face condemnation. True faith, even if it is weak, requires assent to the claim that Jesus died for sinners and rose again from the dead. Without such assent to these historical and theological claims, "respectful" unbelief still qualifies as unbelief.

Others experience mere assent to gospel truth, since they accept the good news without the trust necessary for saving faith. Someone may say, "I believe it's true but I am not ready to act on it." Or, another may profess, "I believe the gospel and I have trusted in Christ as Savior," yet without genuine saving faith. Commonly, we may hear of such that they "profess saving faith without possessing it."

Owen spoke of this reality in the church. In the church there are two types of faith: (1) that which true believers possess, a faith that purifies the heart and works by love; and (2) a mere historical faith that does not justify. Concerning the latter, Owen refers to Simon Magus: "Thus it is said of Simon the magician, that he 'believed,' Acts 8:13, when he was in the 'gall of bitterness and bond of iniquity;' and therefore did not believe with that faith which 'purifies the heart,' Acts 15:9."[4] Such individuals never move beyond knowing and believing the truth intellectually to actually embracing it and the Savior who reveals it.

THE SINFULNESS OF FORMAL INFIDELITY

Rejecting the gospel, whether it involves open denial, superficial attraction, respectful disagreement, or mere assent, is unbelief that must be categorized as sin and first and foremost against God. Any sin against Christ, such as refusing to believe in Him (John 8:45), remains sin against God. When Jesus spoke or worked, God spoke or worked (John 4:34; 5:19–47). So, to reject or dishonor Jesus is to reject or dishonor God (John 5:23). Charnock argued of those rejecting Christ:

It casts a dishonour upon God more than all other iniquities; it is a departing from him after the highest and clearest declarations of his nature, a representation of him under all the disparagements imaginable, and under all encouragements of complying with him. As those that trust Christ are "to the praise of God's glory," Eph. 1:12, so those that distrust him are to the dishonour of his name.[5]

God gave His best in providing His Son for our sins, so rejecting Him is the worst thing we, the worst people, can do. Unbelief against Christ and God spits upon God's best (see Matt. 26:67). Abraham's faith offered glory to God (Rom. 4:20). Unbelief tramples it.

Unbelief, Charnock observed, "fling[s] dirt in the face of all those attributes which were illustrious in the work of redemption: of his wisdom which contrived it, of his righteousness which executed it, of his mercy which is infinitely commended by it, of his truth which is engaged to make good the intent and purchase of it to every one that believes."[6] For the believer, all of God's attributes are a ground for and aid to faith. Everything of God is for us if we believe. Thus, truth of His attributes necessarily strengthens our faith in Him. But unbelief strikes at every attribute, because to assault one is to assault all. "And as there was not an attribute but God intended to glorify in Christ," testifies Charnock, "so there is not one but this sin doth really vilify."[7]

When people malign God's attributes in unbelief, they "undeify" Him and deconstruct who He is. In some sense, theism may be worse than atheism. To claim, "There is no God," is one thing, but to testify, "God is, but He is not good," is perhaps worse. Even without words, those who reject the gospel of the true and living God scream, "God is not good!" Unbelief portrays God as an evil tyrant and robs Him and Christ in the gospel of their peculiar glory, from where His attributes most clearly shine forth. Thus, maintained Charnock, "as our Saviour was tormented by the Jews in every part of his body,—head with thorns, face with spittle, hands and feet with nails, and wholly with reproaches in what was dearest to him,—so is God dishonoured by unbelief in every perfection. As their actions denied Christ to be the Saviour of the world, so the acts of this sin deny God to be the God of the world."[8] The rejection of the gospel and God are one and the same.

Refusing the good news calls God a liar, while embracing it testifies that God is true (John 3:33). Indeed, Charnock claimed, "it is the highest glory a creature can give to the Creator, to acknowledge him a God of eternal and immutable verity.... Now, as the true believer glorifies not only the truth of the Son, but of the Father, so the unbeliever outrages not simply Christ, but God the Father, whose counsels and commands are published by him."[9] We all want others to believe us when we speak the truth. Not believing the gospel puts God and Jesus below even Satan as "the father of lies" (John 8:44). We either affirm God for who He is or deny Him to be who He is.

In the words of Charnock, God can as soon "cease to be, as cease to be true."[10] Charnock added,

> Some say that if God should appear in a human shape, light would be his body, and truth his soul; so essential is truth to the Deity, "it is impossible for God to lie," Heb. 6:18. If we fancy him a liar, we fancy him no God, because we represent him doing a thing impossible to the divine nature, changing an unchangeable goodness into a hateful unfaithfulness. What is his power, knowledge, sufficiency, if truth and faithfulness, the glory of all, be wanting? As sincerity is the beauty of all graces, so veracity and holiness is the lustre of all divine perfections.[11]

All of this is to say, formal unbelief portrays God as the scheming, murderous, and lying devil (John 8:39–45).

God declares, through His Son, the greatest truth and good toward sinners. Indeed to reject this message murders one's own soul, since it came from Him who so humbled Himself that unworthy sinners might be so exalted. There could not be a higher goodness shown toward sinners than the gospel. As God says in Isaiah 5:4,

> What more was there to do for my vineyard,
>> that I have not done in it?

Because God in the best way gave us His best, He could do nothing more, especially while displaying His goodness, mercy, power, and justice.

UNBELIEF IS DEVILISH

Unbelief mirrors the rebellion of the devil in a few important ways. In likeness to God, the devil was originally so glorious, he was the closest of all the angels in bearing. He knew of this preeminence, some argue, but it got the better of him. Charnock related such a position: "And seeing the legions of angels created with him, and himself in the highest rank, he would be singular, subject to none, and ruler over all; choosing rather, says Augustin, to delight in the subjection of others to him, than in his subjection to God."[12] The dignity that he desired belonged to the Son of God alone.

The devil did not wish to be like the other angels, who are "ministering spirits sent out to serve for the sake of those who are to inherit salvation" (Heb. 1:14). Christ possessed what the devil was not promised or even capable of. So, as Charnock noted, the devil "sets himself chiefly against mankind, as having a particular enmity against them, whose dignity in the hypostatical union was envied by him, which was his sin, and the cause of his fall. Men always have the greatest animosity against them, upon whose account and occasion they suffer."[13]

The devil's opposition is connected to his failure to be subject to the Son of God as God-man. Hebrews 1:6 says, "And again, when he brings the firstborn into the world, he says, 'Let all God's angels worship him.'" Was Satan prepared to worship the God-man, Christ Jesus? Did a third of the angels fall because they would not acknowledge God's wisdom and purposes in the giving up of His Son, as God-man, to be Lord and Ruler of all?

Thus, Charnock put the matter so well:

> In all these ways unbelief has a resemblance to the devil's sin. It affects an equality with God in a self-dependence, rests in the sufficiency of its own righteousness, without bowing down the will to the acceptance of grace, delights not in subjection to God, refuses Christ, the head and mediator of God's appointment. In all which pride is signal; and indeed pride of reason, and pride of will, are the two arms wherein the strength of unbelief lies.[14]

God appointed Christ, not Satan, to rule over the heavens and the earth.

Satan has always had a particular hatred toward the Son of God. He experiences not just pride, but also jealousy and envy, murder and lies, and all working against the Son of God and His people. Satan knows he cannot defeat God, but he can try to stop people from believing in the Son of God. And when he does that, he vainly seeks to rob the Son of the glory that he wishes he possessed.

In the wilderness, Satan unsuccessfully tempted Jesus to throw Himself down from the pinnacle of the temple (Luke 4:9). After that, when Jesus was preaching in Nazareth, the unbelief of the people in response to Christ's message was not unlike Satan's methods. The people in the synagogue were "filled with wrath," and they desired to "throw him down the cliff" (Luke 4:28–29). Not only did they not believe, but they acted like their father, the devil. In this way, and many more, the devil opposes Christ, either immediately (i.e., the temptation) or mediately (i.e., through evil people).

Satan is also the father of unbelievers. Speaking to the Jews who opposed Christ, Jesus said, "You are of your father the devil, and your will is to do your father's desires" (John 8:44). This was the case in the beginning. The serpent was a liar and murderer, whom God cursed. Cain's will was to do his father's desires. Cain was a liar (Gen. 4:9) who murdered his brother (Gen. 4:8). As a result, like the serpent, he is cursed (Gen. 4:11). Cain had a father who fell from heaven. But Cain also had many brothers from the same family, such as Judas (John 6:70–71). Unbelief is obedience to Satan and disobedience toward God and Christ.

God is in charge of revealing to creatures how He can do them good and how they should in response serve Him. The devil was not content with the good God showed him and so spurned the service, and thus he did not serve God as he ought to have. He sought his own ways above God's. Unbelief tells God, "I will not receive your goodness; I want my own ways and will serve no one but myself." Unbelief is devilish in this way.

Not only is unbelief a devilish sin, but it is worse than that of the devils. The fallen angels never received an offer of mercy like those who hear and refuse the good news to sinners. As Charnock noted, the devils can say, "We did indeed refuse the cover of the wings of the Son of God. But we never refused a Christ bearing our sins in our nature, for none was offered to us, after the experience of the misery of our first contempt. Can any such plea be made by an unbeliever under the sound of the gospel?"[15] Remember, the Son entered this world not as an angel but a man, with only the latter offered grace and goodness as result. Unbelievers rejecting the gospel slap God in the face profoundly, a sin "more inexcusable than that of devils."[16]

APPLICATION

If you believe in the Son of God for the forgiveness of sins, you have the duty and the blessing to continually praise God for the gift of faith that you possess, for it is faith that gives you courage and helps you overcome anxiety and fear.

By nature, we are not only indifferent but also hateful toward God with a worse-than-devilish unbelief that robs Christ of His due honor. God had every right to leave us in a state of condemnation and misery, but He delivered us from the wrath to come. At one time we only displeased Him, but now we are a pleasure to Him through the gift of faith. He has taken His people from the lowest place and raised them to the highest. To do that, the Son had to descend from the highest place to the lowest. He did not do this for devils, but for humans. Now you can say, with godly pride, "The life I now live in the flesh I live by faith in the Son of God, who loved me and gave himself for me" (Gal. 2:20). That is our daily song.

SIN'S MANIPULATION: I WANT TO BREAK FREE

SELFISH AND DECEITFUL CONTROL

We live in a world—especially in the digital world—where everyone manipulates and gets manipulated. Sometimes manipulators know very well what they do and other times, because the sin becomes so deeply rooted in the heart, they are partially blind to their schemes. But what is manipulation? It is a form of control. Arising out of our sin nature emerges the desire to be in control, which often involves wielding power over others whether physically, mentally, or emotionally.

Manipulation occurs in the harmful influence we exercise on others, sometimes thinking that our intentions and how we carry them out are righteous and good. Yet, in the desire to maintain control, we end up sinfully and selfishly using such tactics as coercion, trickery, lying, complaints, mind games, denial, fake kindness, exaggeration, accusations, murderous threats, comparisons, blame-shifting, guilt-tripping, playing dumb, ridicule, insults, and silent treatment—just to name a few. In summary, manipulation uses whatever means are "necessary" to stay in control over others. Manipulation occurs most frequently in the closest relationships we have. In a rather sinister manner, we feel safer acting this way in more established relationships. In the end, while we may insist or even think we act this way for the best interests of others, we love only ourselves at the expense of and in hatred of others. And we will at times resort to the most underhanded schemes possible in order to get what we want from the other person.

Manipulation is not synonymous with persuasion. A medical doctor may persuade a patient by emphasizing the 95 percent success rate of an operation or medication. In such cases, the doctor genuinely feels this course of action will benefit the patient. Thus, he stresses the positive rather than the negative of the 5 percent failure rate. He can give a legitimate and persuasive "nudge" without selfishness or deceit. The manipulator, on the other hand, may feign or intend such righteous persuasion, yet resorts to coercion either directly or indirectly, most often in a verbal manner and using the tactics mentioned above.

Manipulation may also use also nonverbal tactics and attacks, such as shrugs, tears, sighs, pouts, flops, stomps, faces, gestures, silence, and abandonment. Such abusive measures can easily evolve into worse physically abusive behavior including restraint, physical deprivation, lockouts, slaps, punches, kicks, chokes, and worst of all, deadly assault. Whether verbal or nonverbal; emotional, mental, or physical, the behavior allows manipulators to shape and mold the circumstances to their own advantage to get what they want and govern what they get. For example, we know that flattery works because we are all generally suckers for a compliment. Yet flattery is dangerous precisely because it is a form of manipulation. Even the appearance of kindness can be a form of manipulation. As Iago admits in Shakespeare's *Othello*, "I follow him to serve my turn upon him." Iago deceitfully offers servile obedience and an appearance of loyalty to Othello in order to plot his downfall.

MANIPULATION IN GOD'S WORD

In the garden, before the entrance of sin, the Serpent manipulated Eve with his cunning words, as she attested, "The serpent deceived me, and I ate" (Gen. 3:13b). He wanted control over Adam and Eve and deceived them for selfish reasons. In a sense, they were subject to abuse, yet still responsible for their rebellious choices. Since the Fall, we all by nature have been both the subjects and perpetrators of such satanic manipulation.

The story of Rebekah and Jacob manipulating Isaac and Esau (Gen. 27) reminds us that such a sin occurs even among the people of God under certain circumstances. Incidentally, the deceiver, Jacob, was himself deceived by the manipulative Laban and (possibly also) Leah (Gen. 29:25). Laban devilishly tricked Jacob to marry Leah, making him work seven more years for Rachel, the wife he really wanted (Gen. 29:30).

God's Word provides many examples of manipulation and the untold misery and complications it brings for not only the victim but also the offender. Sin never ultimately wins. Absalom's story warns us of how manipulation can destroy the lives of others and ourselves. This handsome, unblemished young man (2 Sam. 14:25) won over the people with his treacherous scheme to make himself king. He gathered chariots and horses, which was something his father had not done, but apparently something that gave Absalom a royal status. Horses and chariots were associated with Israel's Gentile foes (2 Sam. 15:1). Clearly Absalom was not looking to God or trusting in His name (see Ps. 20:7–8) but acting like a Gentile, doing things the Torah had forbidden or warned against (see Deut. 17:16; 1 Sam. 8:11).

To gain power and control, Absalom manipulated the people of Israel. He was a consummate politician, working hard at first and offering promises of what he would do for the people (2 Sam. 15:2–4). He was prepared to do that which David was not, or so he alleged.

But this was fake news, designed to exalt himself at the expense of his own father. What did Absalom do? He flattered people and made grand promises. He deceived others for selfish ends in order to gain control. In a word, he manipulated: "And whenever a man came near to pay homage to him, he would put out his hand and take hold of him and kiss him. Thus Absalom did to all of Israel who came to the king for judgment. So Absalom stole the hearts of the men of Israel" (2 Sam. 15:5–6).

Absalom manipulated by words and symbols, acting like the king who would truly help and bless people. But he just lusted for power and prestige. Symbols and style usually win over substance in politics, and the case of Absalom proves that.

Delilah emerges as another manipulator leading to the downfall of the mighty Samson (Judg.16). Seeking to control Samson on behalf of the lords of the Philistines, Delilah deceived Samson with false guilt about supposedly failing to love her (Judg. 16:15). Her dogged persistence eventually wore Samson down as he revealed his secret weakness to his beloved yet traitorous woman who handed him over for defeat. The Philistines drained his strength by cutting his hair and then gouged out his eyes (Judg. 16:21). She befriended and seduced him with false affection in order to control him. True love gives, but her love was selfish and no love at all. Samson was still responsible, but he was also manipulated by a woman who knew how to gain control over him. Have we not ourselves learned that revealing certain secrets to certain people can give them control that they later use to their malicious advantage? Opening our hearts can make us vulnerable, which is not necessarily wrong. But we must be wise with our disclosures, which can be used against us for pernicious ends.

False prophets are manipulators, par excellence. Our Lord tells us to beware of such, for they come in sheep's clothing but are in fact ravenous wolves (Matt. 7:15). They fake good intentions to gain an advantage for selfish ends. Paul alerted the Corinthians that this is a tactic from the evil one: "And no wonder, for even Satan disguises himself as an angel of light. So it is no surprise if his servants, also, disguise themselves as servants of righteousness. Their end will correspond to their deeds" (2 Cor. 11:14–15). False teachers serve their own appetites, "and by smooth talk and flattery they deceive the hearts of the naive" (Rom. 16:18). They speak falsehoods, catering to the fleshly side of their listeners, as a way to manipulate them and receive the approval of man (Mic. 2:11).

TYPES OF MANIPULATION

Manipulation comes in many forms in its selfish and idolatrous quest for control and coercion. A villain may play the victim. A false teacher can lead people astray, in the name of the Lord and using His Word (albeit with both distorted) and then cry, "persecution!" when confronted. The true defenders of the faith become the enemies. The villain, manipulator that he is, must preserve his position and reputation at all costs, so he distorts the situation to his advantage as the supposed victim.

Sometimes we are in a position where we want something, but must face the desires and opinions of others. We may exaggerate the advantages of our preferred choice and understate the disadvantages. This was Satan's tactic in the garden (Gen. 3:4–5). We can, like Jacob (disguised as Esau), do a small favor for someone and then "twist their arm" into doing something greater for us (Gen. 27:5–10). When our generosity to others is based purely on what they can do for us, we are guilty of manipulation.

We also, with veiled threats, manipulate people who fail to comply with our wishes. We might also withdraw our friendship, become distant, sulk, or put a guilt trip on others, all of which are meant to leave others wondering, *What did I do wrong?* Children become manipulators at a very young age and can easily take advantage of others by throwing tantrums and screaming bloody murder at the slightest provocation. Or, like adults, they can give the silent treatment.

People very often use money to dominate others. They buy favors, power, and prestige. For example, Simon the magician "believed" (Acts 8:13) but was not content with the promises of the gospel. He wanted more and so offered money to the apostles, saying to them, "Give me this power also, so that anyone on whom I lay my hands may receive the Holy Spirit" (Acts 8:19). Peter exposed the manipulative scheme, but the spirit of Simon lives in many church members who use wealth in hopes of putting the pastor under their thumb or gaining a "controlling interest" in the church.

At bottom, manipulators are selfish people who are unwilling to sacrifice out of love for the good of others. But they are quite willing to sacrifice others for their own ends. Manipulation tramples the command to love your neighbor. This type of sinful self-love will often be accompanied by the violation of several commandments with such practices as false worship, idolatry, taking the Lord's name in vain, lying, stealing, harming, and coveting.

APPLICATION

We are all guilty of the sin of manipulation to some extent. We need to weigh our actions carefully and prayerfully toward others with a view to discovering manipulative tactics. When we fail to trust God, we will turn to trust ourselves. As this happens, we seek to control and dominate others through manipulation. This sin is, like others, first a failure to live under the rule of God.

In addition, we should also be on guard against being manipulated. The world in which we live is a manipulative one. Consider the trappings of social media and the marketing techniques used to trick us and make us slaves of the temporary stuff of life. We are constantly being told in one way or another, "You need more, and you need this particularly, if you truly want satisfaction in life, which you currently don't have, do you?"

Only the gospel of Jesus Christ can raise the manipulated and the manipulator up from the madness and idolatry of control and coercion. God tells us in His Word what is truly important. When we live under His rule, in dependence upon Him, we are in the safest place because we have relinquished sinful self-control, which we never had to begin with. Attempts to control and coerce deny the gospel and its power in Christ. He conquered not by devilish schemes and trickery but by sacrifice and suffering. You want to win someone over? Die to yourself by living for Christ and others. Look to the Lord for change in that person or other areas such as your current financial situation. You do not need to resort to the manipulative cheating of the system, your boss, or others through "dishonest gain" (Jer. 22:17; 1 Tim. 3:8).

Thus, let us by God's grace keep our lives free from the love of money and the tendency to manipulate others to get it. At the same time, may we look to the Lord to teach us contentment (Phil. 4:11) remembering that He gives us what we need and will never leave or forsake us (Heb. 13:5).

Even God, who exercises total control over the universe, does not manipulate us. He does not resort to trickery or deceit. He tells us the truth about ourselves in love so that we can also have a right understanding of who we are. There is no flattery from God: we are sinners, desperately in need of a Savior. Yet He who is perfect in holiness loves us in spite of ourselves. And God's love toward us is not selfish. He gives up His beloved Son to His enemies (Rom. 8:32). Jesus shows the love of God by willingly and joyfully sacrificing Himself for us in order to win us to Him. This is not manipulation because this type of wooing is born out of self-giving, not self-taking. He who so graciously loves us demands that we respond to His love by loving others in the same way. There exists no place for taking advantage of others for our own selfish ends.

The cure for manipulation is to look to God and Christ, who reveal to us that manipulation is the way of the devil. The gospel is anti-manipulation.

SIN'S THOUGHTS: YOU WERE ALWAYS ON MY MIND

THE MIND

"The mind is its own place, and in itself / Can make Heaven of Hell, a Hell of Heaven," so said Satan in Milton's *Paradise Lost* (Book 1, l. 254). Satan's theology is, in the end, wrong, but he does capture the monstrosity of the mind, a place where all types of contradictions and absurdities take place.

One can only guess what a place of beauty Adam's mind must have been before the Fall. He had access not only to the world around him, but also to knowledge of divine things in accordance with God's will. But with the Fall, his assessment of natural man's thoughts is not promising.

God made man in His image and likeness and "very good" (Gen. 1:31). But several chapters on from the calamitous fall into sin, the Lord looked down at the wickedness on earth, noting that "every intention of the thoughts of his heart was only evil continually" (Gen. 6:5). This stunning indictment on humanity at this time in world history brought a worldwide judgment by flood. The punishment fit the crime, the root of which was evil-inclined thinking proceeding from corrupt hearts. Only Noah, "an heir of the righteousness that comes by faith" (Heb. 11:7), and his family were spared.

Yet even those professing to belong to the Lord have come under some searching denunciations concerning their thoughts.

> O Jerusalem, wash your heart from evil,
>   that you may be saved.
> How long shall your wicked thoughts
>   lodge within you? (Jer. 4:14)

In Matthew 9:3, the Jewish scribes were speaking to themselves, claiming that Jesus blasphemed because He forgave the paralytic of his sins (see v. 2). In response, "Jesus, knowing their thoughts, said, 'Why do you think evil in your hearts?'" (Matt. 9:4). Our Lord was quite familiar with the problem of sinful thinking. He later spoke about such, testifying, "For out of the heart come evil thoughts, murder, adultery, sexual immorality, theft, false witness, slander" (Matt. 15:19). Notice that Jesus actually lists the evil and heart-induced thinking first, before other heinous sins. The heart includes, said Charnock, "all the inward operations of the soul, which play their part principally in the heart, whether they be the acts of the understanding, the resolutions of the will, or the blusterings of the affections."[1] Clearly, we need to take the subject of sinful thinking seriously. Indeed, Goodwin rightly recognized the immense task of considering the "Vanity of Thoughts," the very title of his work on the subject, of which he claimed, "would prove of all else the vastest."[2]

THOUGHTS AND THE WILL

Goodwin described thoughts as "all the internal acts of the mind of man, of what faculty soever, all those reasonings, consultations, purposes, resolutions, intents, ends, desires, and cares of the mind of man, as opposed to our external words and actions (Isaiah 66:18)."[3] And when these thoughts arise and "pass through," they usually do so in connection with an affection, such as anxiety, fear, or happiness.

By stating that thoughts arise "usually" related to affections, we affirm that both non-sinful and unwanted intrusive thoughts about sinful things may occur. We live in a fallen world with many evil things before our eyes and deep within our hearts. We process things not simply by sight but by our understanding. The mere viewing of or reflection upon sin is not sinful. For example, witnessing or thinking about someone committing murder does not necessarily mean we have committed a sin, since we can either disapprove or approve of the action. The "intention of the thoughts" from the heart determines the character of the thought (Gen. 6:5).

We may see or think about a sin without necessarily being guilty of the sin. But the moment "the will wills it" (even in the mind and soul), the thinker is guilty of sin. Charnock noted that "thoughts are morally evil when they have a bad principle, [lack] a [proper] end, and converse with the object in a wrong manner."[4] In the case of the good angels, they apprehend the sin that caused the other angels to fall, but they do not know the sin by what theologians call a "practical cognition." Similarly, glorified saints may remember their sins on earth, but only in a way to enhance in their minds the mercy of God, not to delight in such sins. Jesus understood the nature of temptation in His wilderness testing at the hands of Satan (Matt. 4) and what was being offered to Him. Yet He never transgressed, even though His mind apprehended what Satan was (deceitfully) offering. God knows and sees all things with a full knowledge, but His infinite holiness means He cannot sin in His awareness of all the sins of all peoples in all ages. When God, Christ, angels, and glorified saints reflect upon sin, they detest it in a manner appropriate to their ability to hate sin. Saints on earth who possess indwelling sin are capable of such hatred but with an imperfect, though truly renewed, ability.

There arise what some call the "first motions" of sinful thinking, which come from the corruption that is in us, even from remaining sin in true believers. Formal consent or inclination to the corrupt thought may not be immediately present to our mind for it to be a sin. In other words, while a memory of a past sexual sin may not be sin, the person may have a desire arising without realization of such. The heart and mind are deceitful, with many thoughts arising because we lack sufficient holiness to keep them from flowering in our hearts.

The immediate arising of an evil inclination (albeit without recognition) makes the thought sinful. As Charnock argues, "Voluntariness is not necessary to the essence of a sin, though it be to the aggravation of it."[5] We must set certain boundaries for our thoughts, and our failure to guard them is our responsibility before God and His Word. Even when a thought springs up, as it were, without our formal consent, we cannot excuse ourselves if that thought is in violation of God's will. The Christian is to "take every thought captive to obey Christ" (2 Cor. 10:5). When a flurry of sinful thoughts erupts in the mind, we cannot excuse ourselves, even if there is more aggravation in the sin if we dwell on these thoughts and let them "ruminate" in our minds instead of immediately mortifying them at their first rising. Consider Goodwin's remarks: "That even those thoughts, wherein the soul is passive, and which Satan casts in . . . wherein he ravishes the heart, rather than begets them on us (if there be not any consent to them in us . . .), I yield those thoughts are punishments often of neglect of our thoughts, and of our [allowing] them to wander."[6]

These "involuntary" thoughts are often because we fail to "fan into flame the gift of God," which is given to all believers so that we have a spirit of "power and love and self-control" (2 Tim. 1:6–7). But while we should always seek to mortify the first rising of a sinful thought that happens, as it were, "involuntarily," Goodwin said that the more dangerous realm of sinful thoughts lies in the voluntary acts whereby we "ponder and pore, and muse upon things."[7]

Charnock said thoughts are sinful when they have "no lawful object, no right end; [they are] not governed by reason, [they are] eccentric, disorderly in their motions, and [they are] like the jarring strings of an untuned instrument."[8] We can sin with our thoughts in relation to God, ourselves, and others. These may be either sins of omission or commission. We are guilty not only for what we think that is contrary to God's will but also what we fail to think that we ought to when the context demands a certain thought (e.g., rejoicing at the lawful success of a neighbor instead of harboring envy).

DELIGHTING IN VAIN IMAGINATIONS

People can imagine a whole host of evil thoughts, which they do not enjoy in the actual outward acting of the sin. In many instances they do not plan to carry out the act, often for a lack of ability to do so, but they allow their imagination to run wild with lusts of all sorts. Theologians in the past have called this "speculative wickedness." Many people take a lot of pleasure in their fantasies without the fear of shame that comes for those who actually commit such acts.

The Spirit may meet such sinful imaginations with a true horror over what has entered the mind. Or a continued ruminating delight may occur for what is clearly against God's law. Now, it is ordinarily impossible to have an inclination to something without some pleasure, even if it is a small degree. True detestation and hatred of sin, which God and Christ possess, means there is no inclination (and thus delight) whatsoever. Even when we hate sin, we still hate sin imperfectly.

Our inclinations toward sin may begin in seed, so that the smallest hint of sin is about to flower; and we may, by God's grace, abort its earliest beginnings of the thought. But when we take pleasure in the sinful inclination, it brings a greater guilt upon us. Goodwin put the matter gravely: "An outward act of sin, it is but as an act of *whoredom* with the creature when really enjoyed: But this is *Incest*, when we defile our souls and spirits with these imaginations and likenesses which are begotten in our own fancies, being the children of our own hearts."[9] Imagining sin is dangerous because it prepares us for the external act: "Yea," said Charnock, "how many sinful thoughts are twisted together to produce one deliberate sinful word!"[10]

TYPES OF VAIN THOUGHTS

The "speculative wickedness" that remains within even the children of God because of indwelling sin also manifests itself regarding the remembrance of past sins. Goodwin thus spoke of reviving "in our thoughts the pleasure of sinful actions passed; when the mind runs over [past sins] with a new and fresh delight; when men raise up their dead actions long since buried in the same likeness they were transacted in."[11] What we should do, added Goodwin, is "blot them out through faith in Christ's blood," but instead we "copy and write them over again in [our] thoughts with the same contentment."[12] We are sinfully reliving now internally what we sinfully committed externally in the past. Though no one will see it, God knows it to be sin and so must we.

For Christians who genuinely struggle with the remembrance of past sins, we are obliged before God to keep sin from making us "obey its passions" (Rom. 6:12). Since sin does not have dominion over us, we can have victories over our sins instead of letting them gain the upper hand constantly against us.

Our thoughts also need to be governed appropriately. We can even think certain thoughts that are not, in the abstract, sinful, but when we think of them "unseasonably" (to use Goodwin's phrase), we can end up sinning. Speaking "unseasonably" is often forbidden or warned against in the Scriptures (e.g., Job's friends), just as a word spoken "in season" is commended (Prov. 15:23; 25:11).

Vain thoughts denote those occurring in an inappropriate context. "This misplacing of thoughts, suppose they be good," argues Goodwin, "is yet from a vanity of the mind; did those thoughts come at another time, they should be welcome. We find our minds ready to spend thoughts about anything rather than what God at present calls unto."[13] We may be in the middle of praying and suddenly find ourselves thinking about getting to the post office before it closes or when the hockey game starts tonight. We may be listening intently to the pastor preaching on the glories of Christ's love from John 17, only to find ourselves reflecting on finishing the taxes this week or what's for lunch. These are misplaced thoughts, which may not be sin in another context but become such when we should be focusing on something else. To be clear, the sin is aggravated when we know we should be focussing on the sermon but willingly continue to let ourselves think of other thoughts that distract us from God's Word.

Misplaced thoughts can plague any Christian, but they are the consistent pattern of the religious hypocrite. Charnock warned, "A hypocrite's religious services are materially good, but poisoned by the imagination skulking in the heart that gave birth unto them. It is the wicked mind or thought makes the sacrifice (a commanded duty), 'much more an abomination to the Lord,' Prov. 21:27."[14]

Our thoughts may also bring guilt upon us through fantasizing. "Men create fool's paradises to themselves," says Goodwin, "and then walk up and down in them: as, if they had money enough, what pleasures they would have if they were in such places of preferment."[15] Absalom vainly imagined himself as a good king who would take care of people and give them justice. In actual fact, he had no legitimate right to the throne and had no intention of bringing justice (2 Sam. 15:4). We can dress our thoughts up in pretended righteousness so long as we can imagine a future of personal status and glory. "If I were wealthy, I would give lots of money to the needy," says the heart that deceives itself into thinking we would really do it. In fact, we may be just coveting lots of money and wanting to make it look good.

THE DEVIL'S ALLIANCE

We should be aware of the seriousness of vain thoughts. Charnock argues that sinful thinking brings us into "the nearest communion with the devil."[16] For example, jealousy and selfish ambition plunged us into the "earthly, unspiritual, demonic" wisdom from below (James 3:15). There is a battle for our thoughts and affections. Satan would love to dethrone Christ from our hearts. He attacks relentlessly and we sadly give in far too easily.

Judas's betrayal of Christ began in the imagination. But, as John tells us, "During supper, when the devil had already put it into the heart of Judas Iscariot, Simon's son, to betray him . . ." (John 13:2). The plots of Judas to orchestrate the arrest of Jesus were those of a man in deep communion with Satan. As Christians, we do not need to despair that Satan can have dominion in our minds, but that does not mean he cannot influence our minds with his various onslaughts. What hope do we have against such an enemy? When the evil thoughts rise up, and they will, we can find immediate cleansing in Christ and the grace to fight off the mental attacks, for He was the one who did so perfectly. Still, we must remember that it is never fine to delight in evil, even if we never carry it out. Such delight remains a dance with the devil in the presence of Christ, who dwells in our hearts by faith (Eph. 3:17).

APPLICATION

Many of our thoughts are downright wicked, and we would be utterly ashamed if a video of such showed up on YouTube. This should humble us to the core of our being, especially when we are tempted to lift ourselves up in comparison with others. In fact, we are filled with vain thoughts about ourselves, as Goodwin observed in the occasions when we are "proud, self-confident, self-applauding, foolish, covetous, anxious, unclean."[17] Paul noted this of the self-righteous Jews in his time who refused to submit to God's righteousness (Rom. 10:3) and were culpable of vain thoughts about themselves. But even the most irreligious of this world foolishly fantasize about promoting themselves, ignorant of God's will for their lives. As Charnock noted of such, "The most forlorn beggar has sometimes thoughts vast enough to grasp an empire."[18]

Even though sin has no dominion over the Christian, and God gives us good thoughts of Him and His grace, we still struggle with stirring up all sorts of evil in our minds. This is vanity, a striving after Satan. Still, let us be encouraged as Christians, that Christ exhibited the perfect thought life for us as the foundation of our justification and the source and example of our sanctification. Let us likewise rejoice that God has more thoughts toward us of mercy, love, and goodness than we have of rebellion toward Him. We can say with the psalmist,

How precious to me are your thoughts, O God!
How vast is the sum of them!
If I would count them, they are more than the sand.
I awake, and I am still with you. (Ps. 139:17–18)

We are also commanded to bring "every thought captive to obey Christ" (2 Cor. 10:5); and God does not command what He does not give. He gives us the grace to bring our thoughts into subjection to Him, so that we can obey Philippians 4:8, "Finally, brothers, whatever is true, whatever is honorable, whatever is just, whatever is pure, whatever is lovely, whatever is commendable, if there is any excellence, if there is anything worthy of praise, think about these things."

The Lord also gives a clarion call to repentance, which we all need to hear, just as His people of old needed:

"Let the wicked forsake his way,
    and the unrighteous man his thoughts;
let him return to the LORD, that he may have compassion on
    him,
    and to our God, for he will abundantly pardon." (Isa. 55:7)

God abundantly pardons. When we consider how many thoughts have risen up and gone astray during the days of our existence, we should be thankful for the abundant mercies that are shown to us through Christ Jesus. Do not be like the wicked, who have no room in their thoughts for God (Ps. 10:4), but rather think of God often so that good replaces evil.

SIN'S TEMPTATIONS:
I WANT IT ALL

OF THE MAKING OF MANY BOOKS

For the Christian, our battle against temptation comes both from within and without. We face the assaults of the devil, other people, and the world in their various combinations. But we never face these assaults apart from our own inclinations to evil. This makes temptation a subject worthy of serious consideration and explains why many works exist on this topic alone. In the seventeenth century, John Downame (1571–1652) wrote *The Christian Warfare*, a work on temptation and the onslaughts of the world, the flesh, and the devil. Its comprehensiveness can be seen in the more than one-thousand-page 1634 edition. Many other Puritan theologians wrote (not surprisingly) massive treatises on spiritual warfare. One gets the feeling that we would need many more thousands of pages to understand the nature, power, and mystery of temptation.

Many definitions of temptation have been offered, but one can hardly do much better than John Owen, who in his classic work *Of Temptation* (1658) provided this one: "Temptation, then, in general, is any thing, state, way, or condition that, upon any account whatever, has a force or efficacy to seduce, to draw the mind and heart of a man from its obedience, which God requires of him, into any sin, in any degree of it whatever."[1] A temptation either causes or allures us to sin against God by one of two principal ways: allowing evil into or drawing evil out of our hearts. When this happens, we are drawn away from God, which is a spiritual danger.

OUR OWN WEAKNESSES

Despite being spiritual people, we are also still sickly in our souls. In and of ourselves, we are without power to withstand the evil solicitations and thoughts that percolate in our minds and hearts. We drink in temptations like the drunkard drinks in alcohol, always to our detriment.

If we become too confident in ourselves, puffed up with pride, we have already fallen into temptation. Owen vividly remarked, "He that says he can do any thing, can do nothing as he should.... Do not flatter yourselves that you shall hold out; there are secret lusts that lie lurking in your hearts, which perhaps now stir not, which, as soon as any temptation befalls you, will rise, [disturb], cry, disquiet, reduce, and never give over until they are either killed or satisfied."[2] Admitting our own weakness in temptation is one of the means of guarding against falling into temptation, which is why we daily pray: "And lead us not into temptation, but deliver us from evil" (Matt. 6:13).

Temptations come from within, from the heart. Watson said, "The heart is *fomes peccati*, the breeder of all evil. Our own hearts are the greatest tempters (James 1:14)."[3] As Owen wrote, "Temptations and occasions put nothing into a man, but only draw out what was in him before."[4] If Peter could fall into temptation, even in the presence of Jesus Himself, are we safe? Jeremiah 17:9 reminds us that "the heart is deceitful above all things, and desperately sick." The heart seduces us with temptations that are evil, but we either excuse them or we dress them up in righteous clothes to make them more presentable. In actual fact, the suggestions are filthy, like polluted menstrual cloths (see Isa. 64:6).

A temptation toward that which is evil constitutes a leap into the darkness away from the light. The heart turns away from God when one falls into temptation. A temporary rupture of communion with God occurs when we give in to temptation. We can then dangerously think that our behavior has no implications for such communion. Also to our peril, we can go too far in the other direction, believing that God has utterly forsaken us and we have no grounds to be called children of God. Both are dangerous views. Temptations divert the mind from communion with God, but they can also take us away from the gospel solutions for our sin. In other words, temptations take us away from Christ but also take our eyes off of Christ once we fall into them.

Our inward temptations toward evil give, according to Owen, "*oil and fuel* to our lusts,—[they] incite, provoke, and make them [disturb] and rage beyond measure."[5] A certain temptation may be exacerbated by the object and an occasion and so fueled to the point that of feeling like an army presses against us with deadly force. The temptation becomes "wholly predominant," argued Owen, and

> so dealt it with carnal fear in Peter, with pride in Hezekiah, with covetousness in Achan, with uncleanness in David, with worldliness in Demas, with ambition in Diotrephes. It will lay the reins on the neck of a lust, and put spurs to the sides of it, that it may rush forward like a horse into the battle. A man knows not the pride, fury, madness of a corruption, until it meet with a suitable temptation. And what now will a poor soul think to do? His mind is darkened, his affections entangled, his lusts inflamed and provoked, his relief is defeated; and what will be the [outcome] of such a condition?[6]

We are fully responsible for our lusts and temptations within. Any evil from the heart is our responsibility. Owen made an important point:

> Now, when such a temptation comes from without, it is unto the soul an indifferent thing, neither good nor evil, unless it be consented unto; but the very proposal from *within*, it being the soul's own act, is its sin. And this is the work of the law of sin—it is restlessly and continually raising up and proposing innumerable various forms and appearances of evil, in this or that kind, indeed in every kind that the nature of man is capable to exercise corruption in.[7]

A lust or temptation toward something against God's law cannot be "indifferent." We are responsible for our thoughts, desires, lusts, and temptations.

Because of original sin, the seed of every sin still remains in our hearts. We may, because of age, constitution, context, gender, etc., feel the force of certain temptations more than others. A poor young boy may be tempted to steal a candy bar where a wealthy elderly man would not struggle at all, since he no longer enjoys sweets and, even if he did, could afford to pay for them. A teenage boy will ordinarily have greater temptations toward pornographic images than a teenage girl. But whether young or old, poor or rich, male or female, we would still be surprised what is lurking in our hearts, ready to devour us.

Goodwin made the argument that every person is "radically still inclined to [all kinds of sin]; be the constitution of his body what it will," which may not be generally given to certain specific sins, "so as put that soul into another body, it would be as notoriously inclined to them as any other man is."[8] Regarding these inclinations, Goodwin declared, "God oftentimes stops and plugs up the holes as he pleases, that they may not run out at every hole" (see Esth. 5:10).[9] Context, time, circumstance, and other factors account for why a person does not fall into every temptation possible. We do well to remember for ourselves M'Cheyne's famous declaration that "the seeds of all sins are in my heart."[10] We may never carry out something as horrific as a rape or a murder, but the "seeds" are there.

SATAN'S DARTS

Besides our own hearts, Satan is another source of temptation. "Satan never sets a dish before men," said Watson, "that they do not love."[11] He aims to bring dishonor to God and Christ by ruining our souls as far as possible. He is our "adversary," warned Peter, who "prowls around like a roaring lion, seeking someone to devour" (1 Peter 5:8). Peter would know from painful personal experience, wouldn't he?

Temptations from within are made more forceful by the outward temptations that come from Satan. We sin readily even without the assaults of Satan; but he is always on the prowl, ready to attack that we may sin. After all, he is called "the tempter" (Matt. 4:3), whose confidence is such that he would dare to take on the Lord Jesus.

Christians ought to be aware of the power that Satan possesses, but it is a power limited by a sovereign God. Imagine what ruin Satan and the fallen angels would do to God's people if He were not sovereign? The thought is too scary to contemplate. Charnock attested, "The goodness of God makes the devil a polisher, while he intends to be a destroyer."[12] Yet, while Satan is "God's devil," we should not underestimate or be ignorant of his devices (2 Cor. 2:11). "All that Scripture teaches concerning devils," John Calvin warned, "aims at arousing us to take precaution against their stratagems and contrivances, and also to make us equip ourselves with those weapons which are strong and powerful enough to vanquish these most powerful foes."[13]

Satan, as the father of lies, will lead our already deceitful hearts astray with many temptations (Gen. 3:1–5, 13; John 8:44; 2 Cor. 11:3;

1 Tim. 2:14; Rev. 12:9). Although he knows he cannot snatch a true believer from the Father's hand (John 10:29), his storms can help make shipwreck of someone's faith to the point that that person's profession comes under suspicion (1 Tim. 1:19–20). He knows our end will be unspeakable joy, but until we get there, he will aim to make us miserable. Although he is stupid, his intelligence towers above the smartest man in the world. He not only deceives us, but does so craftily as he plays to our individual weaknesses and fancies. As William Jenkyn (1613–85) noted, "He has an apple for Eve, a grape for Noah, a change of raiment for Gehazi, and a bag for Judas."[14]

As noted above regarding personal temptations differing based on age, gender, context, etc., William Spurstowe (1605–66) observed that Satan tempts younger men with sexual fornication, a middle-aged man with "an itch for honor and to be great," and an old man with "covetousness and peevishness."[15] William Gurnall (1616–79) attested that no actress possesses "so many dresses to come in upon the stage with as the devil hath forms of temptation."[16]

Spurstowe related the numerous devices used by Satan to tempt people to sin. Several of these are worthy of our attention if we wish to be aware of his schemes against us. In some cases, the devil will begin with lesser temptations and move to greater ones. We are not as troubled by lesser temptations and so not usually disposed to get out the full armor of God against such a "small" attack. Yet we need the double-edged sword of the Word for even small temptations, not a harmless toothpick of fleshly determination. There is, as Gurnall warned, "a spark of hell in every temptation."[17]

Satan also has specific darts that he fires at us. We are all like Achilles to him and he aims for our most vulnerable spots. He and his demonic host with him can put evil into the hearts of the wicked (John 13:2), but he also tempts with enticements and persuasion: "Then a spirit came forward and stood before the LORD, saying, 'I will entice him'" (1 Kings 22:21). Satan even tried to entice Jesus, claiming, "All these I will give you, if you will fall down and worship me" (Matt. 4:9). Like Delilah relentlessly pressing Samson to bring about his downfall (Judg. 16:16), so the devil persists against us in his quest to destroy us. He continually hurls worthless promises and dangerous delights at us. "Satan promises the best," affirmed Thomas Watson, "but pays with the worst: he promises honor and pays with disgrace, he promises pleasure and pays with pain, he promises profit and pays with loss, he promises life and pays with death; but God pays as he promises, for all his payments are made in pure gold."[18] Our Lord knew that suffering was the way to glory, but Satan's aim was to tempt Christ to bypass such hardships. Sadly, in relation to faith in and fellowship with Christ, many in the church today fail to see the value of adversity and the danger of prosperity. In general, the seventeenth-century Puritans understood this concept well, and as John Geree (1601–49) observed in *The Character of an Old English Puritan, or Non-Conformist* (1646), the Puritan viewed the Christian life as "a warfare, wherein Christ was his captain, his arms, prayers, and tears. The Cross his banner, and his word, *Vincit qui patitur*" (he conquers who endures).[19]

In our temptations, Satan wants us to call evil good and good evil (Isa. 5:20). He clothes sin with the appearance of virtue. Greed is "saving," lust is "love," abortion is "self-care," drunkenness is "medication," and laziness is "rest." Satan makes use of "nice" false teachers, wolves in sheep's clothing (Matt. 7:15), to tempt God's people into doctrinal error. Satan also ensnares us with things that are lawful. Hard work can be a temptation to us who want riches, glory, and honor. Or hard work can keep a father away from caring for his family. Family and friends, work and sports, education and music are all fuels in the engine of Satan's temptations. He does not even need to allure us with something obviously sinful, but can take good things and twist them because we are prone to abuse good gifts.

Satan and his demonic host also tempt us with things that are obviously unlawful. Sometimes he overcomes with wicked thoughts that appear suddenly and ferociously and leave us wondering, *How can I possibly be a Christian and think such awful things?* The world, argued Watson, is Satan's "diocese where he visits; we are sure to find Satan, whatever we are doing,—reading,—praying,—meditating; we find him within, how he came there we know not; we are sure of his company, uncertain how we came by it."[20] This is often the work of the devil who catches us off guard, even in times of prayer or listening to a sermon.

Consider Elijah, who could shut the rains of the sky with prayer, but he could not shut his heart from temptations (1 Kings 19). Spurstowe urged us to be "abundant in the use of prayer," and quoted Bernard of Clairvaux, who observed, "Satan's temptations are grievous to us, but our prayers are more grievous to him."[21] We should never forget the words of our Savior in Matthew 26:41, "Watch and pray that you may not enter into temptation. The spirit indeed is willing, but the flesh is weak." As Owen famously quipped: "He that would be little in temptation, let him be much in prayer."[22] As well, Watson claimed, "Prayer is the best antidote against temptation."[23] The devil hates the darts that we sling back at him and that fly on the wings of Christ's lordship.

THE WORLD'S DANGERS

The apostle John was quite up front about the dangers of the world to the soul. He exhorted his Christian readers: "Do not love the world or the things in the world. If anyone loves the world, the love of the Father is not in him. For all that is in the world—the desires of the flesh and the desires of the eyes and pride of life—is not from the Father but is from the world" (1 John 2:15–16). The desires (lusts) of the flesh and eyes are in us, but the world provides an outlet of temptations for our flesh and eyes.

Owen noted how the world gets into the flesh and eyes, "mixes itself with them, unites, incorporates."[24] Our fleshly desires and the world are friends with each other; they receive mutual encouragement from each other; they feed off of each other.

We must not be conformed to this world, which conformity begins in the heart. The flesh loves the deceits of what the world promises: esteem, satisfaction, happiness, riches, and more. "For what does it profit a man," Jesus asked rhetorically, "to gain the whole world and forfeit his soul?" (Mark 8:36). The obvious answer? "Nothing, it profits him nothing!" The world can offer you everything, but it never gives what it promises while it takes you away from the eternal joy that only the Lord can provide.

But if we are honest, we love the world and feel its temptations a lot more than we are willing to admit. Temptation feeds off of pride. By nature, we think of ourselves more highly than we ought, and so we are tempted, for example, to make a name for ourselves (Gen. 11:4). The world provides opportunities for our flesh, and sometimes we even meet with some apparent success in our quest for worldly glory. We love titles: president, doctor, chairman, etc. But we place little value on the one that matters most in Christ: *servant*. The world offers illegitimate yet tempting shortcuts to what we desire, such as sex before marriage rather than patiently waiting for God's gift on His terms. The marketing world takes advantage of an abundant media platform to burn temptations into our eyes and hearts at an alarming rate each day. We are assaulted each day by a world that tells us we do not have enough and need more. We fall into these temptations, sometimes not even aware we are being sucked in. We give in too quickly to feel any real force of temptation.

APPLICATION

The flesh, the world, and the devil prove to be fierce enemies against us in our ongoing walk with the Lord. In our own strength, we are not only unable to resist temptation, but also frequently unwilling. Unless the Spirit of Christ is working powerfully in our souls, we will fall again and again. The Spirit will preserve us, but He does this divine work through God's ordinary means, yet mysteriously (John 3:8), never "magically." No, we must, in the Spirit, pray to be delivered from falling into temptation, whether that temptation is internal and private or external as the result of various solicitations. Likewise, in the strength of the Spirit, we must fight "the good fight of the faith" (1 Tim. 6:12) by waging war against the enemies that "war against" our souls (1 Peter 2:11) as we face such temptations day after day and hour after hour in each day.

We must lay hold of both God's promises and His ordinary means of grace (e.g., the Word, prayer, and the sacraments) if we are going to arm ourselves for battle. Through these, the Lord conveys to us all we need for our salvation, that we may in this life "grow in grace" (2 Peter 3:18) on our way to glory. Thus, like Christ, we must know and believe God's Word. When He fought the temptations of the devil in the wilderness, He fought them and him in the Spirit and according to the Word of God.

Moreover, the author of Hebrews exhorted us to "lay aside every weight, and sin which clings so closely" as we look to Jesus, "the founder and perfecter of our faith" (Heb. 12:1–2). When we do this, we can be victorious over our temptations. As Paul reminded the Corinthians, "No temptation has overtaken you that is not common to man. God is faithful, and he will not let you be tempted beyond your ability, but with the temptation he will also provide the way of escape, that you may be able to endure it" (1 Cor. 10:13). This gives us hope in our unceasing battle against temptations.

When we, in utter dependence upon the Lord, "submit" to him, we can be "firm" in our "faith" and "resist the devil," who "will flee (James 4:7; 1 Peter 5:8–9). The strength of our enemies as well as our own weaknesses are a grave cause for concern. But God. But Christ. But the Spirit.

17

SIN'S DEGREES:
LITTLE LIES

TALKING OR CRYING?

Are some sins worse than others? The straightforward answer from the Bible, "Yes, of course." However, for whatever reason, some believe that all sins are equally bad in the eyes of God. Notice, this is not the same as saying that every sin, no matter how minor, remains infinitely serious in the eyes of an infinite God and worthy of His infinite condemnation. The Scriptures affirm the latter but not the idea, for example, that stealing a dollar from an elderly woman is just as bad as murdering her. Even those who put forth the equivalence idea understand instinctively that there are degrees of sin. Some really are worse in God's sight than others. When answering the question above, we are able to open up a rich biblical teaching on the doctrine of sin.

For starters, consider the classic text on sin's degrees related to Jesus' sentencing and in response to Pilate: "You would have no authority over me at all unless it had been given you from above. Therefore he who delivered me over to you has the greater sin" (John 19:11). Indeed, as Thomas Watson attested, "Every sin has a voice to speak, but some sins cry."[1] A cold is not cancer, stale milk is not poison, and a bruise is not a broken leg. Likewise, not all sins are as bad as others. But what are the biblical reasons for the degrees of sin?

REASONS

By suggesting that some sins are worse than others, we are saying, with James Fisher (1697–1775), that such "are more abominable, hateful, and offensive to God than others are" (Ezek. 8:6, 13, 15, "greater abominations").[2] True, all sins are hateful and offensive to God, and even the least sin deserves His eternal wrath. But there are biblical reasons that some sins are more heinous than others.

First, there will be differing degrees of punishment for the wicked on the day of judgment. Our Lord's indictment against Chorazin and Bethsaida seems shocking when He claimed that it will be "more bearable on the day of judgment for Tyre and Sidon than for you" (Matt. 11:22). He added that Capernaum will be brought down to Hades and, again, that "it will be more tolerable on the day of judgment for the land of Sodom than for you" (Matt. 11:24). These are stark reminders to people such as those from Chorazin and Bethsaida, who experienced the ministry of Jesus prominently without the response to show for it. Those with greater light offered to them will face a stricter judgment. Their refusal to believe a clear gospel summons is a greater offense than those who did not hear it explicitly preached. The inhabitants of Capernaum suffered from spiritual pride, which evidently blinded them (as pride invariably does) from seeing the glory of God in the face of Jesus Christ. As a result, Sodom, proverbial for wickedness, will be better off than religious Capernaum.

Second, the blasphemy against the Holy Spirit will not be forgiven, but other blasphemies and sins will (Matt. 12:31). The "unpardonable sin" is a notoriously challenging idea to fully understand, but most generally refers to attributing to Satan the work performed by Christ. Such a heinous sin will not be forgiven. Of course, as many have pointed out, this Pharisaic attribution of evil to Christ is probably a set way of responding to Him (a settled heart conviction) rather than simply an occasional utterance against the Lord. Certain Pharisees were calling good evil, and persisting in their hatred against God's Messiah, which means there was no possibility for forgiveness.

Third, following from the idea of presumptuous sins, the Old Testament law made a distinction between unintentional and intentional or presumptuous sin (i.e., with a high hand). In Numbers 15:28–31, the person sinning unintentionally must offer a sacrifice and the priest make an atonement before God for the "mistake" (i.e., sinning unintentionally). Those, however, who sin with a "high hand" are cut off from the people of God because they have openly despised God's Word and commandments. Such a person's "iniquity shall be on him."

RANKING SINS

In his exposition of the Westminster Assembly's Shorter Catechism, James Fisher asked a number of questions that help us understand how sins may be ranked as more or less serious. Some are "committed more immediately against God, or the first table of his law," and so are often more heinous than sins against "any man, or any precept of the second table."[3] By this we mean, speaking blasphemy against God is worse than speaking blasphemy against our neighbor. They are both sins against God, but the aggravation is heightened when directly against God. In fact, even in the second table, we may observe a type of hierarchy. Murder is usually worse than bearing false testimony, unless that false testimony led to the murder of many individuals. Adultery is more serious than stealing, since all adultery involves stealing but not all stealing involves adultery. Coveting another man's wife is not as bad as killing another man's wife.

We must also consider how a particular sin can be aggravated. By aggravation, we mean "something that makes it worse," like a guy

179

who smashes his thumb with a hammer makes it worse by closing it in the car door the next day. So, for example, bitterness of heart is made worse if it occurs during corporate worship. Related to aggravation and ranking sin, Fisher tells us we must consider the following: the one sinning (offender), the one sinned against (offended), the nature of the sin (offense), and the "circumstances of time and place" for the sin (situation). Also, the person's age, abilities, and social standing or office are other factors.[4]

Consider two situations involving theft. First, a pastor steals money from the church offering to pay gambling debts and continue visiting a prostitute. Second, a seven-year-old boy steals a few dollars from another student at school to buy some snacks at lunch. Clearly, the pastor's sin is more serious and aggravated by differences in the categories mentioned above. It is important to remember in our doctrine of sin and its aggravations that "everyone to whom much was given, of him much will be required, and from him to whom they entrusted much, they will demand the more" (Luke 12:48).

We can apply this to so many realms of our Christian living in terms of responsibility. For example, a father, as head of the household, has a greater responsibility to promote godliness in the home than his children do. A pastor has a greater responsibility to promote the truth than his flock.

Our Lord Jesus, who abounded with graces and giftings, had an incredible responsibility to execute the offices of Prophet, Priest, and King as our Redeemer. Theoretically, if He could have sinned, it would have been the most heinous act imaginable. How? Because it would have done more damage to God's glory and honor than if any mere creature sinned against God.

The threats offered in God's Word are instructive for us. For example, willfully skipping church one week is not good, but a continued refusal to attend worship, without being hindered lawfully, is much worse and may be a sign of apostasy from the gospel. The warnings of

Hebrews 10:25–31 to apostates remind us that the most severe New Testament threats we encounter are addressed to religious leaders (see Matt. 23) or professing Christians. A child hitting his brother is not described as one who "trampled underfoot the Son of God" and "outraged the Spirit of grace"; but neglecting to meet together with the people of God is (Heb. 10:24–25, 29).

AGAINST KNOWLEDGE

There are many different avenues of discussion when looking at the various aggravations of sinning. Watson offered several ways in which a person aggravates sins that get to the heart of the seriousness of the topic at hand. Some of these are worthy of consideration. We aggravate or make our sin worse:

First, by willfully and totally neglecting Christian duties: "He is not ignorant that it is a duty to read the word, yet he lets the Bible lie by as rust armour . . . he is convinced that it is a duty to pray in his family, yet he can go days and months, and God never hear of him; he calls God father, but never asks his blessing."[5]

Second, by living in sin that we condemn in others (Rom. 2:1).[6] We must take the log out of our own eye before we can remove the speck from another's eye, or we are hypocrites (Matt. 7:4–5).

Third, by making a solemn vow before God, then breaking it: "Now to sin after a vow, to vow himself to God, and give his soul to the devil, must needs be against the highest convictions."[7] Clearly, it's better not to make a vow at all than break it (Eccl. 5:5).

Fourth, by persisting in our wickedness after being counseled and admonished by faithful friends (Prov. 27:6). God gives us faithful counselors to help us know His will better, and to reject their advice rejects the God who provided it through them.

Fifth, by committing a sin regardless of a specific threat against it (see Heb. 10:24–31): "Yet, though God set the point of his sword to the breast of a sinner, yet he will commit sin. The pleasure of sin does more delight him, than the threats affright him. . . . For men to see the flaming sword of God's threatenings brandished, yet to strengthen themselves in sin, is in an high manner to sin against illumination and conviction."[8]

Sixth, by sinning while under God's chastisement. So, a Christian father may gamble and lose money, get found out, and suffer shame for putting his family in jeopardy. If we find him sitting at the casino after this, his sin would be aggravated. The idolatry of Ahaz took place "in the time of his distress" (2 Chron. 28:22). Yet he continued in his faithlessness before God when he should have turned and repented. So not only sinning while under God's judgment, but also continuing in a course of sinning is worse than the person who sins but repents for the evil committed.

Seventh, by boasting about a sin after indulging in it. Sinning boldly and blatantly is far worse than that occurring in weakness and with repentant weeping after it (see Rev. 22:15; Rom. 1:28–32). Paul highlighted this behavior, even among the Christians in Corinth: "It is actually reported that there is sexual immorality among you, and of a kind that is not tolerated even among pagans, for a man has his father's wife. And you are arrogant! Ought you not rather to mourn?" (1 Cor. 5:1–2).

Eighth, by causing others to sin. Whether a heretic or false teacher who leads people into error, or a boy who gets his brother to join him in vandalizing the neighbor's house, the sin is heightened when we involve others. As our Lord warns, "Whoever causes one of these little ones who believe in me to sin, it would be better for him if a great millstone were hung around his neck and he were thrown into the sea" (Mark 9:42).

APPLICATION

Not all our sins are equally bad, though all our sins are worthy of God's damnation. We ought to consider the context for every sin to determine how bad it is. We live in an age where pastors think they can commit adultery, steal from the church, lie in the process, and take a few months off before returning to the pulpit, "stronger than ever." We need to remember that their standing in the church as ordained officers means their sin cannot be treated the same way as the sins of other Christians. Indeed, they can be forgiven and restored, but we must see how, by virtue of their calling, they must be held to a higher standard, not unlike the politicians who represent us. There are consequences for sin and the more serious the latter is, the more serious the former should be. Sometimes those consequences are not severe, but sometimes they are. There are different penalties for different sins. We do not execute a child who steals a cookie; but a murderer should not be able to say that his sin is no different than the sin of the child who stole the cookie.

By God's grace in Christ our Savior, may we reflect more and more on how we may aggravate our sin. When tempted, let us give consideration, for example, about who we are, whom we are sinning against, and the sin we are committing. May such reflection be a deterrent to sin. May we labor to remember that our identity is in Christ and every sin is committed as a Christian, many times with others' eyes upon us as such. May it matter to us that we sin more grievously against God as our heavenly Father. Finally, remember that, though our sins may be worse than others and we are often more guilty of aggravating sin, we are all great sinners who need a Savior whose grace is greater still. As the hymn "Grace Greater Than Our Sin" testifies, this is a "marvelous, infinite, matchless grace, freely bestowed on all who believe." Indeed, it is a "grace that is greater than all our sin," even the worst.

SIN'S OMISSIONS: WHERE IS THE LOVE?

NO FOOD

When we think of sin, we tend to focus on what God forbids, and neglect what He positively commands. Idolatry takes us away from serving God to ourselves; but it also takes us away from doing good to others.

While certainly not an exhaustive or nuanced definition, as we shall see, the Westminster Shorter Catechism (Q. 14) calls sin "any want of conformity unto, or transgression of, the law of God." Simply, sin concerns failing to do what God commands and doing what He forbids. He says, "Do this," and we don't; and "Don't do this," and we do. In His invective against the Pharisees, our Lord was disturbed that they not only carried out what God forbids, but also failed to accomplish what He demands, and all in violation of God's Word: "Woe to you, scribes and Pharisees, hypocrites! For you tithe mint and dill and cumin, and have neglected the weightier matters of the law: justice and mercy and faithfulness. These you ought to have done, without neglecting the others" (Matt. 23:23). Their failure to be just, merciful, and faithful deserved Christ's condemnation.

At the final judgment, sins of omission will come into focus. Jesus explained that He would rightly send people to hell, "For I was hungry and you gave me no food, I was thirsty and you gave me no drink, I was a stranger and you did not welcome me, naked and you did not clothe me, sick and in prison and you did not visit me" (Matt. 25:42–43). People will enter everlasting torment not only because of what they have done, but also because of what they have not done.

COMMISSION AS OMISSION

The Scriptures are quite clear that Christians not only must avoid sin, but also practice righteousness (Eph. 4:25–32). We cannot hide ourselves in a room (or a monastery) and think we are okay before God because it helps us avoid forbidden pleasures. Our light must shine before men (Matt. 5:16) as we do good works such as showing mercy and making peace in spite of the persecution that comes against us (Matt. 5:9–15). We are called to answer the injustices against us by doing good for those bringing them.

As we learn God's ways and His law, Christians are faced with a greater responsibility to do what is right. James says, "Whoever knows the right thing to do and fails to do it, for him it is sin" (James 4:17). In a sermon preached before the king and queen of England in the late part of the seventeenth century, Edward Stillingfleet (1635–99) said these words of James "have a very [terrifying] consideration in them."[1] Indeed. There are reasons for this. Sins of commission, especially where there are actual sins, are also sins of omission. Thomas Manton observed, "But when we look more narrowly into these things, we shall find both in every actual sin; for in that we commit anything against the law of God, we omit our duty; and the omitting of our duty can hardly fall out but that something is preferred before the love of God."[2] Similarly, Spurgeon said, "In a certain sense, all offences against the law of God come under the head of sins of omission, for in every sin of commission there is an omission—an omission, at least, of that godly fear which would have prevented disobedience."[3]

The distinction between sins of omission versus commission still holds, however. After all, in the case of Eli and his sons, we are told that his sons were acting wickedly ("they lay with the women who were serving at the entrance to the tent of meeting," 1 Sam. 2:22), but Eli was also responsible for not restraining his sons (1 Sam. 3:13).

The Christian life is both a putting off and putting on (Eph. 4:22–24). Our actual sins always involve omission because the violation of a law neglects the positive precept of the commandment(s). If a husband speaks too harshly to his wife, he violates the seventh commandment, and such also involves his failure to speak to her in a gentle, faithful, loving manner of speech. "Husbands, love your wives," exhorts Paul, "and do not be harsh with them" (Col. 3:19). Paul here commands the positive ("love your wives") and forbids the negative ("do not be harsh"). Obviously, not being harsh is a form of love, but the love must go beyond a type of mere silence. So, the argument, "I'm just going to shut my mouth, so I don't say something wrong," neglects the positive injunction of love.

THE SERIOUSNESS OF OMITTING

We are naturally prone to think of the worst sins as those related to something forbidden. Yet in many cases, according to Manton, "sins of omission may be more heinous and damning than sins of commission. They are the ruin of the most part of the carnal world."[4] Stillingfleet brought light to this idea: "We are always bound to have an habitual temper and disposition of mind towards God . . . which is commonly called the Love of God; and is opposed to the Love of Sin."[5] All creatures have a duty to love their Creator, and sin keeps us from such. Yet we remain continually under the positive command, whether we are in or outside Christ. As believers, we alone have the ability, through the Spirit, to fix our thoughts upon God and Christ in fulfillment of the positive duty.

Manton observed how sins of omission harden us more: "Foul sins scourge the conscience with remorse and shame, but [sins of omission] bring on insensibly slightness and hardness of heart."[6] Moreover, sins of omission open the way for sins of commission to take place. Manton added: "They lie open to gross sins that do not keep the heart tender by a daily attendance upon God. If a man do not that which is good, he will soon do that which is evil."[7] Remember, David committed adultery with Bathsheba because of a sin of omission. He should have been fighting God's battles (2 Sam. 11:1). His failure in a duty led to the commission of multiple sins against his God, family, and neighbors. Likewise, sins of commission often facilitate omission as they sap the resolve for righteous behavior. It is not unusual, for example, for those caught up in a particular sin to stop reading the Bible or coming to church since they are quenching the Spirit (1 Thess. 5:19).

Many people in the world even think of themselves as good people, because they have not committed what they consider to be the really bad stuff. Thus, they claim, "I have not killed anyone." They fail to see that less serious sins can also qualify as violations of a particular command. As Jesus told His hearers after citing the sixth commandment, "You shall not murder" (Matt. 5:21), even someone who is angry with his brother will be "liable to judgment" (v. 22). Simply, anger commits murder of the heart. It may not be as heinous as physical murder, but it is still murder. As the Westminster Larger Catechism affirms (A. 135),

> The duties required in the sixth commandment are, all careful studies, and lawful endeavors, to preserve the life of ourselves and others by resisting all thoughts and purposes, subduing all passions, and avoiding all occasions, temptations, and practices, which tend to the unjust taking away the life of any; by just defense thereof against violence, patient bearing of

the hand of God, quietness of mind, cheerfulness of spirit; a sober use of meat, drink, physic, sleep, labor, and recreations; by charitable thoughts, love, compassion, meekness, gentleness, kindness; peaceable, mild and courteous speeches and behavior; forbearance, readiness to be reconciled, patient bearing and forgiving of injuries, and requiting good for evil; comforting and succoring the distressed, and protecting and defending the innocent.

A lack of charitable thoughts toward someone is tied to the sixth commandment and would be a sin of omission.

While not guilty of literal murder, the "good" people above fail to see that the sixth commandment also demands the positive duties, as the Larger Catechism shows here. Thus, we are called to sacrificially "preserve the lives of others" in the good we do for them as in "mild and courteous speeches and behavior" and "patient bearing and forgiving injuries." Failing to do so is sin.

RELIGIOUS OMISSIONS

The story of Daniel inspires us in many ways, but his prayer life in the midst of persecution is remarkable. Daniel knew a decree forbade him from praying to the Lord, but he still "got down on his knees three times a day and prayed and gave thanks before his God, as he had done previously" (Dan. 6:10). He continued his communion with God and did not forsake prayer as a way to give thanks to God. Many omit such prayer and thanksgiving without the threat of death. Daniel prayed, knowing it may cost him his life. It is always better to obey God rather than man (Acts 5:29).

Certain duties really are non-negotiable in the Christian life, and their omission will prove fatal to our walk with God. Prayer should be a daily discipline in the Christian life, especially since we are told to ask God for our daily bread (Matt. 6:11). Repentance, too, is a lifelong habit that only goes away when we draw our last breath. As Stillingfleet argued, "When a sinner is conscious to himself of fresh acts of sin, he is bound to renew his repentance, and the omission of it adds to his guilt."[8] The omission of repentance when we have reason to repent—which is often—is actually harmful to the child of God. Christians need assurance; and repentance, which is a saving grace, leads to assurance that God, through Christ, forgives us our iniquities.

Ignorance of God's Word can also be a sin of omission if it is willful and connected to a general refusal to receive instruction. Christians today in many parts of the world have access to complete Bibles in their own tongue. Yet this great treasure is more often than not neglected and ignored. Saint Jerome (*d*. 420) rightly affirmed,

> I interpret as I should, following the command of Christ: Search the Scriptures, and Seek and you shall find. Christ will not say to me what he said to the Jews: You erred, not knowing the Scriptures and not knowing the power of God. For if, as Paul says, Christ is the power of God and the wisdom of God, and if the man who does not know Scripture does not know the power and wisdom of God, then ignorance of Scripture is ignorance of Christ.[9]

Reading, knowing, and believing God's Word helps us mature in Christ. We need to drink in God's Word and flush out the sinful toxins of fleshly thoughts and temptations. Omitting the study of Christ in His Word opens us to the alluring and often ungodly counsel of the world. This is why neglecting to meet together for worship is so dangerous to our souls. Consider one of the reasons that we need to meet together to worship: "And let us consider how to stir up one another to love and good works, not neglecting to meet together, as is the habit of some, but encouraging one another, and all the more as you see the Day drawing near" (Heb. 10:24–25). Those who neglect corporate worship on the Lord's Day avoid the opportunity to stir their brethren up to love and good works. The omission of this duty (public worship) typically leads to the omission of other duties (e.g., private and family worship and seeking guidance from God's Word through the week). If we are not fed together, we will go hungry; if we do not feed on the Lord's body and blood, we omit a means of grace; if we do not worship God, something or someone else will take His place.

Often we have not defended God's honor, have been cold-hearted toward our Maker, and have not done what was in our power to do as Spirit-filled Christians. We have been cowardly by regarding man's opinion more than God's. Often we have failed to stand for the truth because we love the praise that comes from man more than the praise that comes from God (John 12:43).

Dorothy Sayers highlights well how sloth functions as a sin of omission; the punishment of the other "deadly sins" is sloth: "It is the sin that believes in nothing, cares for nothing, seeks to know nothing, interferes with nothing, enjoys nothing, loves nothing, hates nothing, finds purpose in nothing, lives for nothing, and remains alive only because there is nothing it would die for."[10] Often our sloth and indifference to zeal for God's honor is dressed up as tolerance; but very often sloth is the reason for our lack of righteous, public activity concerning God's name and glory.

APPLICATION

Even a cursory glance at sins of omission should cause a number of reactions from Christians. First, if we are able to have words with God before our death, we probably ought to confess as Archbishop James Ussher (1581–1656) did on his deathbed, "O Lord forgive me, especially my sins of omission."[11]

Second, we should marvel at the obedience of Jesus Christ on our behalf. He not only refrained from sinning during the course of His life on earth, but He was positively obedient to the precepts of God's law. He did not lack in love to God or His neighbor. His righteousness is imputed to us simply by embracing Him in faith. God cannot reject us because we have, through imputation, fulfilled the law as Christ did. His righteousness really is our righteousness. That anyone could think that they can stand before God and enter eternal life on the basis of their own obedience, even in the slightest way, testifies to the marvel of human madness. Our sins are as numerous as the sand on the sea, but Christ's perfect, complete righteousness answers to this predicament. No one else can or will offer you what Christ alone can. Whether you are a Christian or non-Christian, your greatest need is the One who came into the world to save sinners (1 Tim. 1:15).

NOTES

Introduction: Rock You Like a Hurricane

1. Ralph Venning, *Sin, the Plague of Plagues* (London, 1669), 211.

2. Thomas Watson, *The Doctrine of Repentance, Useful for These Times* (London, 1668), 137.

3. Thomas Brooks, *The Select Works of the Rev. Thomas Brooks*, 6 vols. (London: L.B. Seeley & Son, 1824), 1:41.

4. Brooks, *Works*, 1:41.

5. David Clarkson, *The Works of David Clarkson*, 2 vols. (Edinburgh: James Nichol, 1865), 216.

Chapter 1: Sin's Origins: Sympathy for the Devil

1. G. C. Berkouwer, *Sin*, trans. Philip C. Holtrop (Grand Rapids: Eerdmans, 1971), 10–11.

2. Herman Bavinck, *Reformed Dogmatics*, 4 vols., trans. John Vriend, ed. John Bolt (Grand Rapids: Baker, 2006), 3:28–29.

3. Thomas Watson, *A Body of Divinity* (Edinburgh: Banner of Truth Trust, 1974), 140–42.

4. Watson, *Body of Divinity*, 137.

5. Augustine, *The Enchiridion on Faith, Hope and Love*, trans. J. F. Shaw (Washington, DC: Regnery, 1996), 33 (8.27).

6. John Owen, *The Works of John Owen*, 24 vols., edited by W. H. Goold (Edinburgh: T&T Clark, 1850–53), 8:35.

7. John Duncan, *Colloquia Peripatetica: Deep–Sea Soundings*, 5th edition (Edinburgh: R. & R. Clark, 1879), 94.

Chapter 2: Sin's Contagion: Born This Way

1. Thomas Goodwin, *The Works of Thomas Goodwin*, 12 vols., ed. Thomas Smith (Edinburgh: James Nichol, 1861–1866; repr. Grand Rapids: Reformation Heritage Books, 2006), 6:54.

2. Herman Bavinck, *Reformed Dogmatics*, 4 vols., trans. John Vriend, ed. John Bolt (Grand Rapids: Baker, 2006), 3:292.

3. John Owen, *The Works of John Owen*, 24 vols., ed. W. H. Goold (Edinburgh: T&T Clark, 1850–53), 3:168–69.

4. Stephen Charnock, *The Complete Works of Stephen Charnock*, 5 vols. (Edinburgh: James Nichol, 1864–66; repr. Edinburgh: Banner of Truth Trust, 1985), 4:194.

5. Henri Blocher, *Original Sin: Illuminating the Riddle*, NSBT, ed. D. A. Carson (Grand Rapids: Eerdmans, 1997), 84. Quoted in Ted Peters, *Radical Evil in Soul and Society* (Grand Rapids: Eerdmans, 1994), 326, from Reinhold Neibuhr, *Man's Nature and His Communities* (New York: Scribner's, 1965), 24.

6. *The New-England Primer: Improved for the More Easy Attaining the True Reading of English* (Boston: Edward Draper, 1777), 9.

7. Thomas Watson, *A Body of Divinity* (Edinburgh: Banner of Truth Trust, 1974), 144.

8. See Goodwin, *Works*, 10:9.

9. Goodwin, *Works*, 10:10–11.

10. Goodwin, *Works*, 10:12.

11. Goodwin, *Works*, 10:17–19.

12. Owen, *Works*, 5:324.

13. Owen, *Works*, 5:324.

14. On this, see John Murray, *The Imputation of Adam's Sin* (Grand Rapids: Eerdmans, 1959), 43.

15. Owen, *Works*, 5:324.

16. Goodwin, *Works*, 10:15.

17. Francis Turretin, *Institutes of Elenctic Theology*, 3 vols., ed. James T. Dennison Jr., trans. George Musgrave Giger (Phillipsburg, NJ: P&R, 1992), 9.9.17.

18. Owen, *Works*, 5:324.

19. Watson, *Body of Divinity*, 132.

20. John Calvin, *Institutes of the Christian Religion*, ed. John T. McNeill, trans. Ford Lewis Battles (Philadelphia: Westminster Press, 1960), II.1.8.

21. Goodwin, *Works*, 4:154.

22. "Sin," in *The New Bible Dictionary* (Downers Grove, IL: IVP, 1962).

23. Canons of Dort III/IV, Article 1.

24. Canons of Dort III/IV, Article 1.

25. Canons of Dort III/IV, Article 3.

Chapter 3: Sin's Privation: You've Lost That Lovin' Feeling

1. Thomas Goodwin, *The Works of Thomas Goodwin*, 12 vols. ed. Thomas Smith (Edinburgh: James Nichol, 1861–1866; repr. Grand Rapids: Reformation Heritage Books, 2006), 10:85.

2. Goodwin, *Works*, 10:85.

3. Herman Bavinck, *Reformed Dogmatics*, 4 vols. trans. John Vriend, ed. John Bolt (Grand Rapids: Baker, 2006), 3:136.

4. Jeremiah Burroughs, *The eighth book of Mr Jeremiah Burroughs. Being a treatise of the evil of evils, or the exceeding sinfulness of sin. Wherein is shewed, 1 There is more evil in the least sin, than there is in the greatest affliction . . .* (London: Thomas Goodwyn, William Bridge, Sydrach Sympson, William Adderly, William Greenhil, Philip Nye, John Yates, 1654), 11.

5. See Bavinck, *Reformed Dogmatics*, 3:137.

6. Bavinck, *Reformed Dogmatics*, 3:139.

7. Francis Turretin, *Institutes of Elenctic Theology*, 3 vols., ed. James T. Dennison Jr., trans. George Musgrave Giger (Phillipsburg, NJ: P&R, 1992), 9.2.5.

8. Bavinck, *Reformed Dogmatics*, 3:144.

9. Thomas Manton, *The Complete Works of Thomas Manton*, 22 vols. (London: J. Nisbet, 1870), 4:395–96.

10. Stephen Charnock, *The Complete Works of Stephen Charnock*, 5 vols. (Edinburgh: James Nichol, 1864–66; repr. Edinburgh: Banner of Truth Trust, 1985), 2:230.

11. Charnock, *Works*, 2:230.

12. Charnock, *Works*, 2:231.

13. Charnock, *Works*, 2:231.

14. Augustine, "Homilies on the First Epistle of John," in *Nicene and Post-Nicene Fathers*, ed. Philip Schaff (Grand Rapids: Eerdmans, 1956), 7:505.

15. Bavinck, *Reformed Dogmatics*, 3:145.

16. Quoted in Robert Kolb and Charles P. Arand, *The Genius of Luther's Theology: A Wittenberg Way of Thinking for the Contemporary Church* (Grand Rapids: Baker Academic, 2008), 104.

Chapter 4: Sin's Vocabulary: Fade to Black

1. I first learned this from Richard B. Gaffin in his book *By Faith, Not by Sight* (Phillipsburg, NJ: P&R Publishing, 2013).

Chapter 5: Sin's Remains: Hello Darkness, My Old Friend

1. Thomas Watson, *The Beatitudes: Or, A Discourse Upon Part of Christ's Famous Sermon on the Mount* (London, 1671), 73.

2. Watson, *The Beatitudes*, 73.

3. John Haydon, *The Saints Complaint under the Remains of Indwelling Sin. The Substance of Two Sermons on Rom. vii. 24, etc.* 3rd ed. (London: R. Hett, 1770), 8.

4. Samuel Bolton, *The True Bounds of Christian Freedom* (London, 1656), 18.

5. C. E. B. Cranfield, *Romans: A Shorter Commentary* (Edinburgh: T&T Clark, 2001), 157.

6. John Owen, *The Works of John Owen*, 24 vols., ed. W. H. Goold (Edinburgh: T&T Clark, 1850–53), 6:158.

7. Owen, *Works*, 6:159.

8. Owen, *Works*, 6:159.

9. Owen, *Works*, 6:159.

10. See Owen, *Works*, 6:160.

11. Owen, *Works*, 6:161.

12. Owen, *Works*, 6:166.

13. Owen, *Works*, 6:167.

14. John Newton, *The Christian Correspondent; or a Series of Religious Letters Written by The Rev. John Newton* (Hull, East Yorkshire, UK: George Prince, 1790), 78.

15. Owen, *Works*, 6:191.

16. Owen, *Works*, 6:191.

17. Owen, *Works*, 6:193.

18. Alexander Moody Stuart, *Recollections of the Late John Duncan* (Edinburgh: Edmonston and Douglas, 1872), 150.

Chapter 6: Sin's Sorrow: Hard to Say I'm Sorry

1. William G. T. Shedd, *Dogmatic Theology*, Volume 1 (New York: Charles Scribner's Sons, 1888), 175.

2. Thomas Goodwin, *The Works of Thomas Goodwin*, 12 vols., ed. Thomas Smith (Edinburgh: James Nichol, 1861–1866; repr. Grand Rapids: Reformation Heritage Books, 2006), 4:155.

3. Stephen Charnock, *The Complete Works of Stephen Charnock*, 5 vols. (Edinburgh: James Nichol, 1864–66; repr. Edinburgh: Banner of Truth Trust, 1985), 2:140.

4. Charnock, *Works*, 2:140.

5. Goodwin, *Works,* 10:63.

6. Goodwin, *Works*, 10:63.

7. Thomas Manton, *The Complete Works of Thomas Manton*, 22 vols. (London: James Nisbet, 1870–1875), 1:209.

8. Manton, *Works*, 1:209.

9. Charnock, *Works*, 5:394.

10. Andrew Bonar, *Memoir and Remains of the Rev. Robert Murray M'Cheyne* (Dundee, UK: Hamilton, Adams, and Co., 1845), 154.

11. Thomas Brooks, *The Select Works of the Rev. Thomas Brooks*, 6 vols. (London: L.B. Seeley & Son, 1824), 3:392.

12. Brooks, *Works*, 3:392.

13. Thomas Watson, *A Body of Practical Divinity in a Series of Sermons on the Shorter Catechism* (Aberdeen, Scotland: George King, 1838), 779.

14. Charnock, *Works*, 5:391.

15. Brooks, *Works*, 3:397.

16. Brooks, *Works*, 3:394.

17. Quoted in Jonathan Aitken, *John Newton: From Disgrace to Amazing Grace* (Wheaton, IL: Crossway, 2007), 347.

18. John Owen, *The Works of John Owen*, 24 vols., ed. W. H. Goold (Edinburgh: T&T Clark, 1850–53), 2:152.

Chapter 7: Sin's Alternative: Hurts So Good

1. Jeremiah Burroughs, *The eighth book of Mr Jeremiah Burroughs. Being a treatise of the evil of evils, or the exceeding sinfulness of sin. Wherein is shewed, 1 There is more evil in the least sin, than there is in the greatest affliction* . . . (London: Thomas Goodwyn, William Bridge, Sydrach Sympson, William Adderly, William Greenhil, Philip Nye, John Yates, 1654), 3.

2. Burroughs, *Evil of Evils*, 2.

3. William Gurnall, *The Christian in Complete Armour* (London: Thomas Tegg, 1845), 590.

4. Burroughs, *Evil of Evils*, 4–5.

5. Burroughs, *Evil of Evils*, 18.

6. Burroughs, *Evil of Evils*, 18.

7. Burroughs, *Evil of Evils*, 36.

8. Burroughs, *Evil of Evils*, 43.

9. Burroughs, *Evil of Evils*, 43–44.

10. Richard Sibbes, *The Complete Works of Richard Sibbes*, 7 vols. (Edinburgh: James Nichol, 1863), 1:47.

Chapter 8: Sin's Secrecy: I Put a Spell on You

1. Richard Sibbes, *The Complete Works of Richard Sibbes*, 7 vols. (Edinburgh: James Nichol, 1863), 1:145.

2. Stephen Charnock, *The Complete Works of Stephen Charnock*, 5 vols. (Edinburgh: James Nichol, 1864–66; repr. Edinburgh: Banner of Truth Trust, 1985), 1:479.

3. Obadiah Sedgwick, *The Anatomy of Secret Sins, Presumptuous Sins, Sins in Dominion, & Uprightness* (London, 1660), 8.

4. Sedgwick, *Anatomy of Secret Sins*, 8.

5. John Bunyan, *The Pilgrim's Progress: From This World to That Which Is to Come* (New York: R. Carter & Bros., 1860), 51.

6. Sedgwick, *Anatomy of Secret Sins*, 9.

7. Thomas Watson, *A Body of Practical Divinity in a Series of Sermons on the Shorter Catechism* (Aberdeen, Scotland: George King, 1838), 793.

8. Sedgwick, *Anatomy of Secret Sins*, 13.

9. Sedgwick, *Anatomy of Secret Sins*, 14.

10. Sedgwick, *Anatomy of Secret Sins*, 11.

11. Sedgwick, *Anatomy of Secret Sins*, 14–15.

12. Sedgwick, *Anatomy of Secret Sins*, 16.

13. John Milton, *The Poetical Works of John Milton*, 4 vols. (London, 1842), 2:45.

14. Sedgwick, *Anatomy of Secret Sins*, 20.

15. Sedgwick, *Anatomy of Secret Sins*, 22.

16. Samuel Stanhope Smith, *Sermons on Various Subjects* (London: Printed for J. Mawman, 1801), 303–04.

Chapter 9: Sin's Presumption: Highway to Hell

1. Thomas Manton, *The Complete Works of Thomas Manton*, 22 vols. (London: J. Nisbet, 1870), 4:396–97.

2. Obadiah Sedgwick, *The Anatomy of Secret Sins, Presumptuous Sins, Sins in Dominion, & Uprightness* (London, 1660), 54.

3. Manton, *Works*, 21:341.

4. Sedgwick, *Anatomy of Secret Sins*, 54.

5. Sedgwick, *Anatomy of Secret Sins*, 58.

6. Sedgwick, *Anatomy of Secret Sins*, 58.

7. Manton, *Works*, 21:343.

8. Manton, *Works*, 21:344.

9. Manton, *Works*, 21:344.

10. Manton, *Works*, 21:345.

11. Manton, *Works*, 21:346.

12. Manton, *Works*, 21:351.

13. John Owen, *The Works of John Owen*, 24 vols., ed. W. H. Goold (Edinburgh: T&T Clark, 1850–53), 3:343.

Chapter 10: Sin's Pride: Stand Tall

1. Rebecca Konyndyk DeYoung, *Glittering Vices* (Grand Rapids: Baker, 2020), 21–25, 26, 31, 112, 237.

2. Archibald G. Brown, *Sermons Preached at Stepney Green Tabernacle . . . 1868–9* (London: D. Francis, 1879), 73.

3. Brown, *Sermons Preached at Stepney Green Tabernacle*, 73.

4. Richard Newton, *Leaves from the Tree of Life* (London & Edinburgh: William P. Nimmo, 1878), 102.

5. John Calvin, *Institutes of the Christian Religion*, trans. Ford Lewis Battles (Grand Rapids: Eerdmans, 1986), 1.1.1.

6. C. S. Lewis, *Mere Christianity* (New York: Simon & Schuster Touchstone edition, 1996), 109.

7. Thomas Watson, *The Godly Man's Picture, Drawn with a Scripture-pensil* (Glasgow: John Robertson, 1758), 174–75.

8. Brown, *Sermons Preached at Stepney Green Tabernacle*, 73.

9. Benjamin Franklin, *The Autobiography of Benjamin Franklin: 1706–1757* (Chicago: The Lakeside Press, 1903), 139.

Chapter 11: Sin's Selfishness: All You Need Is Love

1. Thomas Goodwin, *The Works of Thomas Goodwin*, 12 vols., ed. Thomas Smith (Edinburgh: James Nichol, 1861–1866; repr. Grand Rapids: Reformation Heritage Books, 2006), 10:218.

2. Stephen Charnock, *The Complete Works of Stephen Charnock*, 5 vols. (Edinburgh: James Nichol, 1864–66; repr. Edinburgh: Banner of Truth Trust, 1985), 1:223.

3. Charnock, *Works*, 1:224.

4. Thomas Manton, *The Complete Works of Thomas Manton*, 22 vols. (London: J. Nisbet, 1870), 12:68.

5. Charnock, *Works*, 1:224.

6. Charnock, *Works*, 1:224.

7. Richard Sibbes, *The Complete Works of Richard Sibbes*, 7 vols. (Edinburgh: James Nichol, 1863), 4:183.

8. Charnock, *Works*, 1:225.

9. Goodwin, *Works*, 10:302.

10. Goodwin, *Works*, 10:302–03.

11. Charnock, *Works*, 1:224.

Chapter 12: Sin's Envy: Hey Jealousy

1. John Milton, *The First Book of Milton's Paradise Lost*, translation and notes by John Hunter (London: Longman, Green, Longman and Roberts, 1861), 7, emphasis added.

2. Harvey Newcomb, *A Practical Directory for Young Christian Females*, 10th ed. (Boston: Massachusetts Sabbath School Society, 1833), 196.

3. Newcomb, *A Practical Directory for Young Christian Females*, 196.

4. Newcomb, *A Practical Directory for Young Christian Females*, 196.

5. Newcomb, *A Practical Directory for Young Christian Females*, 196.

6. Newcomb, *A Practical Directory for Young Christian Females*, 196.

7. Thomas Watson, *The Godly Man's Picture, Drawn with a Scripture-pensil* (Glasgow: John Robertson, 1758), 69.

Chapter 13: Sin's Unbelief: Losing My Religion

1. Thomas Goodwin, *The Works of Thomas Goodwin*, 12 vols., ed. Thomas Smith (Edinburgh: James Nichol, 1861–1866; repr. Grand Rapids: Reformation Heritage Books, 2006), 10:231.

2. Stephen Charnock, *The Complete Works of Stephen Charnock*, 5 vols. (Edinburgh: James Nichol, 1864–66; repr. Edinburgh: Banner of Truth Trust, 1985), 4:220.

3. Charnock, *Works*, 4:220.

4. John Owen, *The Works of John Owen*, 24 vols., ed. W. H. Goold (Edinburgh: T&T Clark, 1850–53), 5:71–72.

5. Charnock, *Works*, 4:231.

6. Charnock, *Works*, 4:232.

7. Charnock, *Works*, 4:233.

8. Charnock, *Works*, 4:233.

9. Charnock, *Works*, 4:233.

10. Charnock, *Works*, 4:234.

11. Charnock, *Works*, 4:234–35.

12. Charnock, *Works*, 4:267.

13. Charnock, *Works*, 4:267.

14. Charnock, *Works*, 4:268.

15. Charnock, *Works*, 4:271.

16. Charnock, *Works*, 4:271.

Chapter 15: Sin's Thoughts: You Were Always on My Mind

1. Stephen Charnock, *The Complete Works of Stephen Charnock*, 5 vols. (Edinburgh: James Nichol, 1864–66; repr. Edinburgh: Banner of Truth Trust, 1985), 5:289.

2. Thomas Goodwin, *The Works of Thomas Goodwin*, 12 vols., ed. Thomas Smith (Edinburgh: James Nichol, 1861–1866; repr. Grand Rapids: Reformation Heritage Books, 2006), 3:510.

3. Goodwin, *Works*, 3:510.

4. Charnock, *Works*, 5:290.

5. Charnock, *Works*, 5:291.

6. Goodwin, *Works*, 3:511.

7. Goodwin, *Works*, 3:511.

8. Charnock, *Works*, 5:292.

9. Goodwin, *Works*, 3:520.

10. Charnock, *Works*, 5:299.

11. Goodwin, *Works*, 3:522.

12. Goodwin, *Works*, 3:522.

13. Goodwin, *Works*, 3:516.

14. Charnock, *Works*, 5:299.

15. Goodwin, *Works*, 3:523.

16. Charnock, *Works*, 5:300.

17. Goodwin, *Works*, 5:292.

18. Charnock, *Works*, 4:462.

Chapter 16: Sin's Temptations: I Want It All

1. John Owen, *The Works of John Owen*. 24 vols., ed. W. H. Goold (Edinburgh: T&T Clark, 1850–53), 6:96.

2. Owen, *Works*, 6:104–05.

3. Thomas Watson, *A Body of Practical Divinity, In a Series of Sermons on the Shorter Catechism* (Aberdeen, Scotland: George King, 1838), 740.

4. Owen, *Works*, 6:169.

5. Owen, *Works*, 6:110.

6. Owen, *Works*, 6:110.

7. Owen, *Works*, 6:194.

8. Thomas Goodwin, *The Works of Thomas Goodwin*, 12 vols., ed. Thomas Smith (Edinburgh: James Nichol, 1861–1866; repr. Grand Rapids: Reformation Heritage Books, 2006), 10:65.

9. Goodwin, *Works*, 10:66.

10. Robert Murray M'Cheyne, *Memoir and Remains of the Rev. Robert Murray M'Cheyne* (Dundee, Scotland: William Middleton, 1846), 154.

11. Watson, *A Body of Practical Divinity*, 772.

12. Stephen Charnock, *The Complete Works of Stephen Charnock*, 5 vols. (Edinburgh: James Nichol, 1864–66; repr. Edinburgh: Banner of Truth Trust, 1985), 2:364.

13. John Calvin, *Institutes of the Christian Religion*, ed. John T. McNeill, trans. Ford Lewis Battles (Philadelphia: Westminster Press, 1960), 1.14.13.

14. Cited in I. D. E. Thomas, comp., *The Golden Treasury of Puritan Quotations* (Chicago: Moody, 1975), 76.

15. William Spurstowe, *The Wiles of Satan* (1666; repr. Morgan, PA: Soli Deo Gloria, 2004), 61.

16. William Gurnall, *The Christian in Complete Armour: A Treatise of the Saints' War against the Devil* (1662–1665; repr. Edinburgh: Banner of Truth Trust, 2002), 1:382.

17. Gurnall, *The Christian in Complete Armour*, 2:76.

18. Thomas Brooks, "Heaven on Earth" in *The Works of Thomas Brooks*, ed. Alexander B. Grosart (1861–1867; repr. Edinburgh: Banner of Truth Trust, 2001), 2:322.

19. John Geree, *The Character of an Old English Puritane or Non-conformist* (London: Printed by A. Miller, 1649), 6.

20. Watson, *A Body of Practical Divinity*, 740.

21. Spurstowe, *The Wiles of Satan*, 90–91.

22. Owen, *Works*, 6:126.

23. Watson, *A Body of Practical Divinity*, 775.

24. Owen, *Works*, 6:113.

Chapter 17: Sin's Degrees: Little Lies

1. Thomas Watson, *A Body of Practical Divinity in a Series of Sermons on the Shorter Catechism* (Aberdeen, Scotland: George King, 1838), 457.

2. James Fisher, *The Westminster Assembly's Shorter Catechism Explained* (Philadelphia: William S. Young, 1840), 139.

3. Fisher, *The Westminster Assembly's Shorter Catechism Explained*, 140.

4. See Fisher, *The Westminster Assembly's Shorter Catechism Explained*, 140.

5. Watson, *A Body of Practical Divinity*, 458.

6. Watson, *A Body of Practical Divinity*, 458.

7. Watson, *A Body of Practical Divinity*, 458.

8. Watson, *A Body of Practical Divinity*, 458–59.

Chapter 18: Sin's Omissions: Where Is the Love?

1. Edward Stillingfleet, *A Sermon Concerning Sins of Omission Preached before the King and Queen at White-Hall, on March 18th, 1693/4* (London: Printed by J. H. for Henry Mortlock, 1694), 3.

2. Thomas Manton, *The Complete Works of Thomas Manton*, 22 vols. (London: J. Nisbet, 1870), 10:102.

3. Charles Spurgeon, *Spurgeon's Sermons*, Volume 14:1868 (Woodstock, ON: Devoted Publishing, 2017), 379.

4. Manton, *Works*, 10:103.

5. Stillingfleet, *A Sermon Concerning Sins of Omission*, 9.

6. Manton, *Works*, 10:103–04.

7. Manton, *Works*, 10:104.

8. Stillingfleet, *A Sermon Concerning Sins of Omission*, 10.

9. Jerome, *Commentary on Isaiah Prologue* (CCL 73), 1–3.

10. Dorothy L. Sayers, "The Other Six Deadly Sins," in *Letters to a Diminished Church: Passionate Arguments for the Relevance of Christian Doctrine* (repr. Thomas Nelson, 2004), 98.

11. Alan Ford, *James Ussher: Theology, History, and Politics in Early-Modern Ireland and England* (Oxford: Oxford University Press, 2007), 271.

"WHAT IS GOD LIKE?"

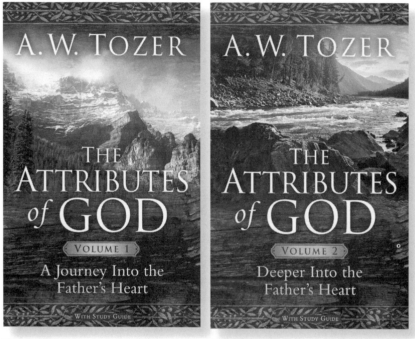

978-1-60066-129-7   978-1-60066-791-6

MOODY
Publishers®

From the Word to Life®

For A. W. Tozer, there is no question more important. In fact, Tozer's desire to know God and His fullness consumed his entire life and ministry. Steeped in Scripture and filled with the Spirit, Tozer preached with striking clarity and power. The sense of his sermons comes through on every page, bringing the Word of God to bear upon you.

also available as eBooks

Some people make theology complicated.
Here's what you need to know.

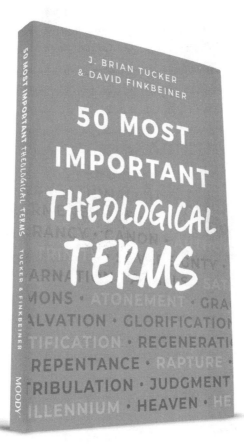

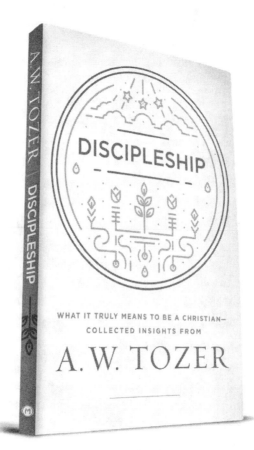